STIRRINGS

Essays
Christian and Radical

EDITED BY
JOHN J. VINCENT

London EPWORTH PRESS

7162 0265 4

Enquiries should be addressed to
The Methodist Publishing House
Wellington Road
Wimbledon
London SW19 8EU
Printed in Great Britain by
The Garden City Press Limited
Letchworth, Hertfordshire SG6 1JS

All Royalties from the sale of
this book are being donated to
the Urban Theology Unit Sheffield.

CONTENTS

Prologue / Stirrings in the Christian Camp   7

1. God as Possibility / *John J. Vincent*   15
  1. The Impossibility of God as Gospel for Contemporary
     Christians   15
  2. The Possibility of God Through Jesus   18
  3. The Possibility of God Through Faith-life   23
  4. Contemporary Stories and the Possibility of God   26
  5. Possibility as God   29

2. Faith as Story / *John D. Davies*   33
  1. Theology and Storytelling   34
  2. Five Gospel Stories of Faith   36
  3. Abraham as Model of Faith   40
  4. Who are the People of Faith?   43
  5. Story as Creator of Future Faith   45

3. A Jubilee and Disciples / *Edward S. Kessler*   47
  1. Jesus 'Avoids the Issues'   47
  2. The Real Issue: a Jubilee   50
  3. Rewards in the Life of the Disciple Group   52
  4. Risks in Discipleship   55
  5. Theological Training for Disciples   58
  6. In the Church   61
  7. In the World   65

4. Inner City Incarnation / *Roy B. Crowder*   69
  1. A Piece of Incarnation   69
  2. Action and Reflection   72
  3. Being with Jesus   74
  4. Proclaiming the Gospel   78
  5. Making Sick People Better   81
  6. Taking up the Cross and Following   82
  7. Proof-texting or Gospel-living?   85

5. Story and Liturgy / *Donald Tytler*   89
   1. Resurrection and Testimony   89
   2. Obstacles and Options   90
   3. Secular Worship   91
   4. Alien Forms   93
   5. Symbols—and God   95
   6. Purging the Symbols   99
   7. Free to Celebrate   101

6. Christian and Radical / *John J. Vincent*   105
   1. A Christ-centred Radicalism?   105
   2. The Jesus Story   107
   3. Theology as Action-theology   109
   4. Faith as Action-commitment   112
   5. God as Predictate   114
   6. Politics as Gospel Action   116
   7. Liturgy as Gospel Rehearsal   118
   8. Making Disciples   120

Notes on Authors   123

Note on the Urban Theology Unit   127

Stirrings in the Christian Camp

'We're ahead of our own thinking.'
  'People are into things they have no theology for.'
The speaker is an evangelical, working in an inner city, commenting on Conferences of Evangelicals at work in the city.

'The theology they taught me never expected anything to happen.'
'I've forgotten all my theology—it wasn't relevant anyway'.
The speakers are ministers reporting on themselves at the start of an Urban Ministry Course in Birmingham.

'We have to start creating a new theology out of what is happening.'
'There are bits of theology we can get into now.'
The speakers are people from overseas who have come together for one of our Easter Theological Conferences.

There are stirrings in the Christian camp. People are discovering ways to live the Christian gospel in a time of theological confusion and disbelief. They are discovering a few things they need, and not missing a mass of things they have forgotten.

Let me come clean. I think there is a new theology around. It is not yet clear. It is not yet systematic. It is not yet in a state to meet all possible objections. It is not yet ready to take on more established theologies. But there is a new theology stirring to be born. And there is a new theology appearing, basically because there are people with authentic Jesus stories to tell, who cannot tell them within the confines of former theologies. And there is a new theology around, equally, because people seem able now, in our time, to find or hear or get into new elements in the central story. These they find to be elements which have lain dormant for a time, but which are intrinsic to the records of Jesus and his first followers. So that from the side of contemporary experience, and from the side of contemporary gospel study, a few new things are beginning to be said. And they are being said by all kinds of people, from all kinds of theological camps.

Two elements, I believe, are characteristic.

First, there is an insistence that what is done shall be *Christian*. No one *needs* to use the Christian story, or the Christian tradition, or Christian people or groups, to explain his existence or his commitment. But those who wish to use the word 'Christian' ought (or so it is felt) to be producing something which relates to Christ in some way —and in some way different from much established theology.

So, secondly, there is an insistence that what is done shall be *radical*. There is room for an evangelical, a catholic, a liberal, or a middle-of-the-road understanding of Christianity. But some now wish to see the place of a possible Christianity which is thoroughgoing, radical and rooted in a fundamental self-authenticity. Not radical in the sense of the 1890s or 1960s, which meant simple Marxism or simple atheism but radical in a basically Christ-centred way which means opening up the stories anew, to ask new questions of them.

Our effort to get to this has a short history, but one worth recording. In Easter 1971, a group of younger theologians came together during the Durham meetings of the Society for the Study of Theology. They agreed to keep in contact and to see whether there was any kind of common feeling between them as to what needed to be said in the contemporary theological scene. In June 1971, I wrote to about twenty, whose names had been agreed, inviting their participation. I wrote:

'In discussions with a number of people over the past six months, the idea has emerged of getting together a series of essays by some younger theologians who seem to be making sense at least to each other.

Negatively, we are agreed on the dead ends from the sixties— Biblical Theology, Theology of Hope, Process Theology, Death of God Theology, Secular Theology, Counter Culture Theology, Logical Positivism, Ontological Theology (what else?—or do some of us live here still?)

Positively, we are agreed also on certain characteristics of the new search we feel ourselves to be engaged upon:

1. The need for a *positive* radical theology, which states belief in God and Christ in terms of personal, interpersonal, social and political actuality.

2. The need for a *British* Radical Theology (Pragmatic?), learning from German and American Radicalism, but not being dependent on them.

3. The need to express a new spirit of preparedness to live positively with *both Christ and Humanism.*

4. The need to express the *Action-Theology* that activates many post-renewal radicals in the ministry, the churches and para-church units.'

The response from several was an immediate, 'No, you may not count me in.' One wrote : 'I still hope for much from the theologies you dismiss.' Another wrote: 'I do not like the idea of a British response—the future is with the Continent and America.' Someone else confided: 'I do not want to be mixed up with radical theology— there is no place for it in my university.'

From the positive responses, three two-day meetings were called. The common position was discussed, and became both modified and elaborated, with everyone putting their own gloss upon it. Seventeen papers were discussed, several of them being revised more than once. A number of them were then used, introduced by their authors, at the Study Weeks on Contemporary Theology, held by the Urban Theology Unit in Sheffield at Easter 1973, 1974 and 1975.

The announced themes were: 'Contemporary Theology' (1973), 'A Contemporary Search for Gospel' (1974), and 'Sociology of Theology' and 'Para Church Theology' (1975). The 1973 and 1974 Conferences have been reported in detail, with pieces by Colin Tatton (Birmingham), David Blatherwick (Warrington), James Logan (Washington, D.C.), John D. Davies, Donald Tytler and myself.[1]

These occasions themselves pushed the debate along further, as will appear in the last chapter. Finally, the axe descended on all but five of the essays, which I think hang together at the same time as approaching the themes from different points of view. An essay by Alistair Kee on 'Transcendence Today', had to be omitted at the last minute, as its material is in a forthcoming book.[2]

What to call ourselves? At first, we chose 'New Soundings' as a title for our modest enterprise, but in the end it seemed to claim too much. We have no great enthusiasm for any label, particularly a theological label like 'Christocentric radicalism'. But 'Christian Radicals' or 'Christ-centred radicals' is the label that most nearly describes us. We certainly do not wish to create a new 'party'. But people will undoubtedly want to put some label on us, so we might as well try one on and see what happens.

Where will other people 'place' us? Our origins, and thus our ideas, place us outside the mental mood of *Soundings.*[3] Our theology is done out of engagement in the contemporary city, not the university. Our hopes are rested, not on conceptions, but on commitment. We believe the basic problems of Christianity come from contradictory lifestyle rather than contradictory reasoning. *Christ, Faith and History*,[4] a more literal successor to *Soundings*, remains unquestioningly academic and Anglican. Like its authors, however, we remain preoccupied with what can be done with the Jesus stories in the Gospels. Perhaps unlike them, though, we feel the urge to experiment *practically* as well as theoretically. We find theology and christology being reforged 'at the bottom', out of contemporary Christian commitment, community, and secular existence, and we find much Gospel study still far behind in sensing it. In this way, we are rather more like the writers of *Seeds of Liberation*,[5] though our origin is in the Protestant, main-line, middle-class churches of Britain, rather than the left-wing Catholic student circles of the U.S.A. But, like them, we think there are some new stories to tell—and some theological conclusions to be drawn. Our stories are very different, though.

So, in terms of accuracy, we had better be 'placed' on our own. We want to affirm the 'group theology' done by the others, and beg now to be heard as one more attempt, like the rest, to put down the way things are, or the way they seem to us to be.

Our essays are part of an ongoing quest. The Urban Theology Unit, which financed us when necessary, holds two Study Weeks on Contemporary Theology in the fortnight before Easter each year. The subjects for 1976 are 'Doing Theology' and 'Theology in Urban Industrial Mission', and that for 1977 is 'Discipleship: Jesus, the Early Church, and Today', followed by a week on 'Theological Directions Now'.

Our grateful acknowledgement is made for permission to quote copyright material as indicated in the notes at the ends of chapters.

Urban Theology Unit   JOHN J. VINCENT
Pitsmoor Study House
210 Abbeyfield Road
Sheffield
S4 7AZ
January 1976

Notes

1. 'Search for Gospel', *New City*, 6 (Sheffield: Urban Theology Unit 1974).
2. Meantime, see a few remarks on pp. 114–5, below.
3. Alec R. Vidler, ed., *Soundings: Essays Concerning Christian Understanidng* (London: Cambridge University Press 1962).
4. *Christ, Faith and History: Cambridge Studies in Christology*, ed. Stephen Sykes and J. P. Clayton (London: Cambridge University Press 1972).
5. *Seeds of Liberation*, ed. Alistair Kee (London: SCM Press 1973).

STIRRINGS

STIRRINGS

ONE

God as Possibility

1. The Impossibility of God as Gospel for Contemporary Christians

Ten years ago, an influential layman said: 'I need the hour of worship in order to get through the rest of the week.' A year or two ago, he altered it: 'I need the rest of the week in order to survive the hour of worship.' A decade ago, we agreed, 'Just don't sing the bits you can't agree with.' A decade later, we ask, 'What will happen if we only sing the isolated bits we can agree with?' Ten years ago, it was generally agreed that there were some hymns you didn't sing. Now, my wife's statement that there are about eight hymns she can sing regularly brings forth the astonished, 'Which eight?' Ten years ago, there seemed still hope that the old God could perhaps stage a come-back if we only found new ways to state the eternal truth. Now, thousands of books on popular theology later, we are asking what on earth the eternal truth can be. In the sixties, ministers could still be upbraided that if they prayed more, visited more, preached better, and organized more wisely, they could all have happy, thriving churches like they have at the seaside and in suburbia. In the seventies, ministry emerges as the faint but available privilege of binding up wounds, acting out parables, hinting at impossibilities, confirming insignificances. In the sixties, the Christians could still wade in behind an establishment God, high and lifted up, who created, preserved, judged, or forgave as he pleased, but was yet to be revered, and honoured, in every possible way, and on every possible occasion. In the seventies, the Christians divide into those who gather still in the surviving places where the old liturgies, or preachings, or theologies, can still be enjoyed in the decency and propriety of estab-lished religion—the 'remnant' of the glorious past—and into those who hardly know where to gather, or how to do liturgy, or preaching, or theology.

For these latter, 'God', as being the name for everything that twenty centuries has established as the core and object and meaning of the Jesus-event, is utterly impossible. They find, as Bonhoeffer did, that they seldom wish to use the word, however much 'outsiders' wish them to. They feel that the style and action of Jesus completely reject

15

the notion of a God 'up there' or 'out there' or 'inside there' who can be held in the mind and toyed with as a philosophical concept. They sense that they stand with Jesus against the God of Christianity or Christendom. They would sooner be called atheists than allow the unutterable mystery that Jesus is and is to them to be prostituted in the service of man's need for self-justification and self-assurance, which are both represented by the idea of 'God'. They find no need to think of a 'personal God', and make no sense of the demand that they should 'believe' that 'he' is 'there'. Indeed, they would go further: the vital issues of personal and corporate vocation, intention, style, and action are not in their experience focused in the God-problem, but rather diverted in it. And the Jesus dynamic, which is concerned with these things, becomes itself diverted by being necessarily attached to the old, impossible God idea. I believe that there is hope for God as possibility, if we will stay with the 'Stirrings' which this contemporary style of faith is beginning to make. But that will only emerge when we have seen the impossibility of the old God.

Alistair Kee's *Way of Transcendence* sees this, but leaves two most serious problems. First, Kee has to posit the existence of something, somewhere, called 'the way of transcendence'. He wishes this 'way of transcendence' to function for theology in the same way as the old idea of God functioned. It is 'that which is incarnated in Jesus', it is 'that which stands over against Jesus', that which compels him and upholds him. But it really is asking a lot that modern man should suddenly become willing to believe in a 'way of transcendence' functioning in these ways, when he found it impossible to believe in God functioning in these ways. Kee rightly claims that his theology retains all the truths of the old theology—simply because he has, in one sense, put a new name to the centre around which all the old theological formulations were made.

The second problem is this. Jesus called God 'Father', and lived his life out in the consciousness, which was undeniably real to him, that there was a divine presence over against him, calling him, anointing him, empowering and judging him. Even though, as has been frequently shown in the last decade, Jesus appears to have systematically taken over the attributes and actions of God, yet still he seems to have 'believed in God'. Now, it is arguable that such a 'belief in God' has to be dispensed with in the twentieth century, just as belief in walking on the water, or in physical resurrection, or in literal ascension, or in the earthquake at the crucifixion, had to be dispensed with in the past hundred years. In this case, it is simply another piece of conceptuality which has cumbered men's minds, from which they can now be freed. But what really is to be made of Jesus's looking beyond himself to one calling him? It is one thing to admit that what he was being called to—an imminent end of all things—just never happened; in this case, God is simply a disappointment. But it is another thing to venture both to discount this whole external-regarding view of Jesus, and also to venture to give it another name, the 'way of transcendence'. Some way must be found to take more seriously the style of Jesus as a secular man living 'before God', as Bonhoeffer says. That is, we must face the total radical secularity of Jesus as the man acting as if all the secrets of heaven and hell, of the Eternal and the Father, are to be found in him. He who has seen Jesus has seen the Father; but what then has he seen?

I think that we must not prematurely seek to end modern man's inability to deal with the God idea either by putting a new name to it, or by denying that Jesus looked beyond himself to someone or something calling him. What we need is a way of saying enough but not too much, a method of communicating without deceiving, which will allow us to live with the Jesus style, in all its utter mystery and utter secularity, while at the same time neither giving in to the traditional conceptual formulations nor settling too soon for premature new formulations. In a sense, it does not matter whether you call what Kee is describing 'transcendence' or 'immanence' or 'mystery' or 'value'. Since we only have the incarnation of it to go on, why not just get on with what we have to go on, and leave aside the question for a while of what is being 'incarnated' in it? Purely as a matter of sensible policy in our present dilemma, this seems to me to be the obvious way through; or at least the most possible way for us to remain men of faith in the present situation.

Thus, living with the impossibility of God in our decades does not mean that we withdraw into middle-class suburban garden culture or humanistic nihilism. On the contrary, living with the impossibility of God allows us perhaps for the first time to begin to experience the odd, unpremeditated, scandalous, irrational, contradictory phenomenon which the early Christians called *pistis*. For *pistis* is not properly translated 'faith', in the sense of 'belief'. It is more properly translated 'trusting', 'venturing', 'abandoning'. To 'have *pistis* in God' did not mean to arrive at a satisfactory notion concerning an ultimate being. It meant to be prepared to risk your existence on the slender hope that the reality vindicating Jesus would vindicate those found 'in him'.

In other words, living with the impossibility of God is the way whereby contemporary man may be able to live 'in Christ'. Of course, at every step, the man attempting to do this will look like a madman, on the one hand to those secure in the old belief that there is an external Being, who can be personally loved, adored, worshipped, and with whom one can have a relationship in terms of obedience, comfort, stability, or judgement, and on the other hand to those completely outside the old faith, who live happily in the sense that 'what you can see is all there is'. To create and live in a ground in between these two well-established and reliable frameworks will be no easy task. But one thing persuades me that the task is not only obligatory but also possible, open and vital. It is that *many people are already living in this no-man's-land between God-faith and no-faith*. They have experienced the Gospel as liberation from mere superficial worldliness; and they have also experienced the Gospel as liberation from self-satisfying God-talk. But they go on naming the name of Jesus. They go on looking to 'the life in Christ' as the meaning of existence. They go on seeking and living in the community that surrounds Jesus's words and works. They already experience 'the impossibility of God' as a kind of gnawing frustration and disappoint-ment. They might perhaps be helped to see it as the Gospel which liberates them into new ways. So the task is urgent—and full of grace already.

2. The Possibility of God Through Jesus

For Christians, Jesus is the prime evidence for God. The list of seven classical 'proofs' can establish an eternal, omniscient, omnipresent, omnipotent, benevolent and providential 'divine being'. But they can-not establish 'the God and Father of our Lord, Jesus Christ'. Indeed, from the beginning, the Christians' God was seen to be in conflict with the sort of God that was posited by others, be they first-century Jews or Greeks; and, perhaps, twentieth-century establishment 'believers'. So that there is nothing new in the suggestion that followers of Jesus may have to repudiate the name 'God', in order to bring that reality to light which is pointed to by Jesus. Indeed, we may say that it has become vital that we lose the name of 'God' in order to be authentic to the Jesus-event. Jesus is the evidence for the Christian God. Is he in fact evidence for any such thing as men historically, and men in general today, have given the label 'God' to? If he is not, then in the name of Jesus, we must cease to speak of God—at least until it is possible to speak it again with its radical Christ-centred meaning.

In other words, there is no way of pointing to Jesus once one has first established 'God'. Educators have discovered it. You spend time proving that God exists, or that God works in history, or that God has a chosen people, or that God works through science, or that God is love, or acceptance, or judgement, or eternity, or the ultimate, or whatever. Then, having 'prepared the way', you try to bring Jesus in. But it never comes off if you are true to the Jesus story itself. For the Jesus story is the story of the systematic and intentional rejection of all the established conceptions and expectations of God. That which Jesus serves—the kingdom of God/heaven—reverses all men's hopes, expectations, presuppositions, and intentions. It reverses man's hope of being significant, and the wish to be involved in significance, by declaring that men deal with the kingdom only indirectly, in the concrete, in the neighbour, in the secular; also that even there, the kingdom cannot be intentionally encountered. It reverses the hope that men can be 'with God', as his conscious, intentional servants, by thrusting the whole question of acceptance far away into the arena of future judgement—a judgement in which those who think they are 'inside' find themselves outside, and those who think they are 'outside' find themselves inside. It reverses the whole vast scheme of human religion, by locating the kingdom thoroughly within the secular. It negates the theories of providence by asserting the indiscriminate nature of creation. It denies men's longing for 'spiritual reality' by declaring that soul-saving is a far-off event, dependent on 'losing life for my sake and the gospel's'.[1]

Therefore the 'Secular Christ' of the Gospels demands a Secular 'God' to whom it all points. But can this 'God' ever be put into the old wineskins of the established God of Christendom, which has become the 'high God' rejected in Judaism, the 'philosophical ground of all things' rejected in crucifixion, the 'God of majesty and power' obliterated in the servant washing the disciples' feet? *Can that radically secular and radically revolutionary 'happening' which we know as the Jesus-event be helped at all by being linked with what men still call 'God'?*

Now, to demand that Christianity in the future shall proceed to do its theology (thinking about God) solely on the basis of Christology is to demand that we do today what the New Testament in fact did. In order to claim that Jesus and the Jesus events were the secret of all things, the New Testament writers said that 'God has made him both Secular King (*kurios*) and Divinely Anointed (*messias*), this Jesus whom you crucified'. That is, the direction in which the New Testament had to go in order to claim total significance for Jesus was the God-direction. They had to declare the ultimate and complete meaningfulness for all men for all time of the things that had been said and done by Jesus by placing the Jesus figure within the schemes of divinity, cosmology, and history which were then current. But

19

this does not mean that we have to take over that scheme in order to say that Jesus for us and for all men *now* is to be described as Son of God, or Word, or Lamb, or any other of the ninety-three titles of Jesus in the New Testament. Neither does it mean that in order to attribute significance to Jesus, we have to place him within the then or now current conventional God-scheme. We have to begin now to do the radical theologizing which the New Testament scarcely began—to begin to discover how in secular terms to say that Jesus is 'Lord of all'. We have to go back to the Jesus event itself, and discover new lines which can be determinative for our belief, in the absence of an agreed or accepted God-scheme, or in the presence of an existing God-scheme in which it is impossible to say the Jesus story at all.

The fundamental evidence for Christian existence is thus the same —it is Jesus. But the deductions about ultimates, or history, or 'God', were either false or were right for their time but are false for ours. We must thus go back to the base line of Christian faith, which is the Jesus-event, and get new lines which can issue in Christ-existence now, just as the placing of Jesus within the contemporary God-scheme made Christ-existence possible then, even if it transformed it into something far less distinctive and paradoxical than it properly is.

What we now have to do is to proceed on the Jesus-event in the same direction as Jesus himself began to proceed. We have to see the Jesus story, not as a paradigm of eternity, or the future, or of 'God', but as a paradigm of that which actually operates within secular existence for the wholeness of humanity and the redemption of history. We have to 'demythologize' so far as the 'externals' are concerned, but we have to 'remythologize' so far as the 'insights into the secular' are concerned. We have to discover *of what* Jesus is evidence today. To what does the Jesus-event point? What is the 'gap' previously valued as 'God-shaped', within human consciousness, which Jesus comes to fill, and regarding which Jesus comes to reveal full and final significance? As Jesus saw ultimate significance (the kingdom) in secular events, so we must see ultimate significance in a hidden dynamic at work in everything, at all times, in every place.

Thus, 'remythologizing' is not an evacuating theology but an *escalating theology*. We do not say less than the New Testament when we do not see the need to relate the Jesus-event to the cosmology-theology of the time. Indeed, we say more than the New Testament when we take the secrets of Jesus and ask how they are working as hidden leaven within man's total secular existence—his behaviour, his love, his commitment, his housing, his 'sense of the important', his compassion, his politics, his career, his ambition, his sacrifice, his communality, his solitariness.Theology from being the old 'queen of the sciences', trying to claim that she smiles on all because all must 'ultimately' feed her and sustain her sovereignty, becomes the 'slave of the sciences', raising unaskable questions, ferreting out the presuppositions behind existence, operating within the no-man's-lands between the disciplines, pressing the hidden significance of every assumption, action and judgement. Theology comes into her own as the secular discipline of asking what the Jesus-events, the Jesus-words, the Jesus-thing, the Jesus-dynamic, actually could mean as a living and operative revolution ('kingdom') within men's lives, relationships, business, families, communities, social groups and national histories.

It may perhaps be worth adding, as an aside, that it does not seem to me that the way *theologically* for this escalation of Christology as a secular dynamic to gain expression will be either easy or straightforward. It would mean following Wolfhart Pannenberg's 'Christology from the bottom', but then reversing the direction, so that one did not then posit divinity on the basis of the Christology (which, as we have seen, would be a vast improvement), but rather posited significant humanity, history, and existence on the basis of the Christology; only when this had been done could one once again perhaps return to the 'universalizing' in a cosmic-theological sense. It would mean following with sympathy the steps of the culture-theologians, but insisting that there must be some kind of Christocentric core to their operations, rather than simply (to be slightly unjust to Harvey Cox) secularity in Jesus when secularity is on the go, festival-fantasy in Jesus when men tire of secularity, religion when men persist in religiosity.[2] It would mean listening sympathetically to other faiths, politics and worldviews, but then insisting that the Jesus-event itself is also a secret understanding of what is going on in history and existence (like Buddhism, or Marxism, or Maoism).

Driving Christology into the secular is fulfilling the distinctive drift of the secular Christ of the New Testament. It is perhaps to follow, in some sense, the way in which 'secular' men of our time can become disciples—though it is a question of presenting the radical unacceptability of Christianity within the secular, so that men cannot avoid seeing it, rather than allowing them to 'dismiss' Christianity because it is based on an odd and unacceptable God-scheme.

But does it ultimately open out the 'possibility' of God? I believe it does. I believe that if we would only allow ourselves to let the Christ-event release us from the old God-scheme, and then allow the Gospel to create in us new, secular understandings, then finally it is

21

inevitable that we shall want to universalize and cosmologize and theologize on the basis of the dynamics we discover revealed within human existence. God will emerge as possibility, but it will be a new God. It will be 'the God the Father of Jesus', discovered anew, or for the first time, by our patient and self-effacing disappearance into the dirt and grime of history, into the ghetto of the small, unseen kingdom ecclesia-community, into the mysteries of 'what make men tick' and 'what men live by' whether by the Name or by any other name. Out of it we shall discover what Jesus is, and what we are, and we shall then again be able to shout with the utterly unjustified and unacceptable boldness and impertinence of the early Christians, that 'Jesus is God'—that the lowest is the highest, that the humiliated is the exalted, that the nothing is the everything, that the little Jesus-group praying holds the stars together, that the parables of the Jesus-people are the leaven of all history, that the cradling in a manger is the God of Gods and King of Kings and Lord of Lords, is Very God of Very God.

Only then shall we see the 'system' of belief, or understanding, which can make sense and hold sense and conviction for ourselves, and possibly even for others. But there is great danger that we shall never see it happen. For we shall hold on to the old conceptuality, even though we see it no longer acceptable to ourselves or to others. We shall think that at least for man to have a non-Christian notion of God is better than for him to have no notion of God at all. We shall not want to lose the residual elements of the 'age of belief', of 'national religion', of 'God' in 'Thought for the Day', at the coronation, at school assembly, at blessing the fleet or the babies. But I think we would better serve the future of man, and of faith, by leaving these old relics of past non-faith (and perhaps what buildings, personnel, money and interests the old 'believers' or status-quo preservers wish to hold on to). Doubtless a national 'God' will be imposed on the semi-believers all round us, and this will leave the Christians to get on with their own business—which of course is really all humanity's business, but which cannot be done while we remain within the totally unacceptable God-scheme that national religion—or even popular religion—demands.

At the end, the God and Father of Jesus would come back, or come in for the first time. Of course. For the truth of Jesus is the truth of everything. It's just that God has to come as possibility again, before he can come as certainty. God has to come as incarnate again, before he can come as eternal. God is possible again if we will retire with Jesus for a century or two into the reality which Jesus claimed his own in incarnation.

3. The Possibility of God Through Faith-life

Fundamentally, Christianity has always been faith based on a few lines of evidence, such as Jesus plus 'signs following'. Faith has been leaping to create the Father on the basis of the unquestionable phenomenon of Jesus and the unquestionable phenomenon of Christian existence. Therefore, for Christians the possibility of God in the future rests, as it does now, upon what is coming from the New Testament, plus the witness of persons in the 'Christ Life'. It is 'religious experience', as seen through the 'Christ-event'.[3]

This simple truth is obscured by the insistence that we must be 'faithful', by which is meant 'loyal to the past', and prepared to go on repeating formulations and creeds which are not ours, but which belong to 'the tradition'. This is to fail to see that 'the tradition' is really no more than a mass of pieces of Christ-life which have been in their time existential and meaningful for people living with the Jesus story, but which were then ossified into systems after they had ceased to be living phenomena. This is true of the 'variety of experience' in the New Testament itself. It is true of much sacramentalism or passion-devotion. It is true of the sin-deliverance theology of the Book of Common Prayer or of Charles Wesley's hymns. All arose as magnificent manifestations of particular ways of reflecting on Christ-existence, which in their own time adequately reflected (or so one must hope) people's real feelings. But their repetition in our time obscures the fact that today *we are the tradition*. If there is nothing new coming out of the Jesus-existence of men today, then there is no tradition, and it will not do for us to go on repeating the old formulations long after they have ceased to be life-giving, or remotely reflective of our Christ-existence now.

(i) New Testament Rediscovery

So the possibility of God as a living option for the future *hangs upon the discovery of significant Jesus-existence now*, as much as it does upon the historical and Christological discovery of the essence of the Jesus-event in the New Testament. But the discovery of the essence of the Jesus-event in the New Testament is, in fact, itself inseparable from the discovery of the varieties of faith-life recorded or reflected there. Here, however, we are in even more uncertainty. We can agree upon the importance of seeing the writings as socio-cultural manifestations of the faith-life of specific historic and localized groups. But we do not know the groups or their situations. We concede likewise that there is a wide pluralism within the New Testament, and that the use of common words does not mean the existence of common concepts. But we can only speculate on what this or that actually meant here or there. We argue the possibility that this or that writer reflected living Christians whose life-style reflected a view of Jesus as a zealot, or a revolutionary, or a suffering servant, or a Davidic messiah, or as 'the day of the Lord', or as a prophet, or as a rabbinic teacher, or as Wisdom, or as Logos, or as Light, or as the personification of the kingdom, or as the philosopher, the saviour, the redeemer, and so on. But we cannot relate these often mutually contradictory notions, much less build a systematic theology either of Jesus or of discipleship upon them. We may see, with Maurice Wiles, 'the specialness of the events, rather than the special way in which the divine action was understood to be operative in them' as most fundamental.[4] But we may not be final about what 'the events' were, as we only know them in their (to the writers) 'specialness'.

Many who would concede all this feel it to be a far healthier situation than one in which a supposed 'unity' was read into every verse. If we are delivered from premature generalizations, we are at least also delivered from premature delineations of what is acceptable and what is not acceptable, of what is 'heresy' and what is 'orthodoxy', what is 'the central development' and what is 'peripheral'. Rather are we faced with a considerable amount of deeply fascinating material, coming out of we know not what socio-cultural milieu, carrying we know not what hidden meanings and implications.

At least, in this situation, the New Testament student concludes that, whatever the multitudinous and singular ways adopted to say it, these writers were trying to say essentially one thing. They write because they believe that there is something about Jesus that has to be said, and it has to be said so that everyone, whatever he thinks about, wherever he lives, whatsoever conceptuality he has, sees this Jesus happening to be decisive, significant, and ultimate. The words used to say it are mutually contradictory, widely diverse, and frequently confusing. But the contradiction, diversity and confusion is because the writers were fundamentally trying to use mere words that happened to be around to describe what was not words at all, but a *fact*, a *happening*, a *thing*, which was centred on Jesus. The very pluralism of the New Testament reveals the impossibility of normality, and also the necessity and possibility of seeking for an 'essence' behind it all: which I take to be (for shorthand here) 'the Jesus Thing'.[5]

The Christian faith-life now has to be formed against the background of a pluralistic document recording pluralistic forms of faith-life. From the outset, therefore, pluralistic kinds of faith-life can be expected. What differentiates the Christian faith-life from others is finally the individual or the group which is willing to see the Jesus story, or part of it, as operative, illuminative, judgemental and significant for them now.

(ii) Christian Existence Rediscovery

When we turn to the 'Christian existence' end of the matter, there is a similar need for looking at matters in a new way. Here again, it has been assumed that the New Testament gives a uniform or systematic answer; and this we must now say was mistaken. This is perhaps worth stressing in a couple of instances, centred on 'Faith' itself.

First, 'faith' has too often not been understood in terms of existence, commitment, or venturing. Rather it has frequently been taken within conventional Christianity that 'faith' was the primary and essential 'belief in God', which then became the basis for action. But now, 'faith' must be seen as the *action*, which then becomes the basis for belief. If 'belief' is primary, then the whole vast machinery of organized Christian churches is always prior to faith and necessary for faith—authorized teaching, catechism, membership training, disciplines, religious experiences, regular sacraments. They are not understood as 'ends in themselves', but as means whereby 'belief' is confirmed, so that action is eventually released. This whole system seems today so often to have crumbled—partly because it is so exhausting and time-consuming that the faithful Christian has no time left for the action. Now, the process must be reversed. Action itself is the place where the Christian becomes 'in Christ', and there is only need for worship or fellowship or study in the aftermath of the revelation within the action, and the emergence within the action of 'faith' as an attitude of commitment and engagement. 'Acting in faith' becomes the prime evidence for the Jesus way of interpreting life—and thus, finally, for the 'existence' of a 'God and Father' of Jesus. The lines of Christian 'faith' are thus drawn from the commitment, from the committed community, from the action.

Secondly, the Christian story about faith and evidence has been reversed. Previously, faith and commitment led people on to 'belief in God'. Now, we cannot be so sure. We must allow the Jesus faith and commitment to lead us where it will. The indications from the Jesus story which in the past led people confidently on to God do not lead all of them there today. 'God and Father' emerge as possibility only where we are content for a time for the Jesus phenomenon to be the location of the faith and commitment, without it leading on to 'belief in God' necessarily. Indeed, in so far as 'God' is this 'high God' of popular myth and culture, it is unlikely that the life of in-Christ action will be thought to point as evidence to the existence of such a 'God' at all. The spectacle of serious people joyfully committed to 'the Jesus Thing', and living for it in small communities of faith, will only provide evidence for 'God' if the God thus conceived of is the supporter of such commitment and community. It may be argued, I think correctly, that the biblical 'I will be there as I will be there' ('I am that I am') is such a 'God', at least at his best. But that may carry little or no conviction to many others, equally committed.

Living with the Jesus story, and faith-commitment to it, are thus the two vital elements. *The God-question must be allowed to arise as one possible implication of this contemporary Jesus-life.* It may not be the most natural, the most characteristic, or the most widely affirmed. Whether the *name* of 'God' is used or not may depend upon questions of personal, social, cultural or national history. It may depend upon questions of expediency, or tactics, or evangelism. Where it helps the Jesus people to 'be themselves' and 'do their Jesus Thing' to refer themselves and would-be followers to the latent or traditional 'God' concept within humanity, they will do so. But where such reference would merely obstruct the radical commitment to new humanity with unnecessary or harmful recollections of the old 'high God', they will prefer to be more unspecific about who or what 'the Father' is, to whom the deeds, style and commitment in Jesus point.

The radical Christian disciple of the secular Jesus is ultimately the only *ground* for the acceptance of the Christian view of things. The fact of his own 'being in it' is the only 'proof' to himself. Perhaps this is the 'witness of the Spirit within' for which Wesley strove! The fact of his 'being in it' is the only 'proof' to others.

Hence, the bits of commitment, community, life-style, vocation, self-denial, self-fulfilment, judgement, mercy, and love beginning to appear anew among Christian groups, in churches and para-churches are part of the way in which faith can become possible for Christians today—and perhaps for others, today and tomorrow. The Gospel story in fact is being used by a vast variety of different groups, to affirm, explicate or judge their own 'thing'—from the pentecostal charismatic movement to the radical Christian movement, to name only two which seem to me to be specially significant. Through them, Jesus becomes a 'live option' again, or for the first time. Beyond that, all things, including the Father, are possible.

4. Contemporary Stories and the Possibility of God

I cannot begin to do justice here to the wide variety of situations and groups within which Jesus language is becoming possible and necessary again. The choice in this volume of one or two places and people is due to the community of study in which I live and work—a community of study which in some sense at least exists for and because of certain 'soundings' in the city, heard by disciples as echoes of Jesus.

Roy Crowder will tell of gospel elements in the life of an Ashram Community House. The Ashram Community as a whole (not mainly community house residents, of course) is similar to the growing number of para-church institutions in our time.[6] The Community now has four inner-city Community houses, where five to eight people in their twenties live together for a number of years. They operate with a two-fold purpose: first, to create a mini-ecclesia; second, to operate as a caring group within a neighbourhood. They see their existence in the light of the synoptic gospels, especially St Mark. In his essay, Roy Crowder mentions specific elements within the gospel story which he sees reflected in the life of his Community house.

The use of the gospel story in this way is not new. Indeed, it was one of the hallmarks of the theology of humanistic care and human reconciliation which arose out of the servant-theologies of the 1960s. What seems to me to be new is the concept of the small disciple group rather than the Church as the agent. From the outside, one can but observe that people who are living this kind of existence are manifesting today many of the characteristics of faith in the New Testament. They look towards Jesus as the origin and meaning of their life together; they are prepared to act on the basis of appearances even when disappointed; and they form among themselves a vital community of mutual dependence, openness, and economic sharing. All of these characteristics they share in varying degrees with other similar commune-type organizations. But, equally, they manifest them in common with the earliest Christian community and similar Christian communities through the ages.

The question that is raised by such stories is at least in part the question, What might a man look like who 'believed in God'? That is, what is the human, secular, materialistic, relational appearance of men and women who wished to set the justification of their existence entirely outside the normal requirements and expectations of religion, family life, career, vocation, economics, etc? If there is to be belief in God, there must at least be people manifesting so radically different a style of life as to force the conclusion that there must be 'another element' in existence or in experience, which could 'explain' phenomena which are so radically other than normal experience.

In the past, such 'para-normal' manifestations have usually been looked for in the sphere of *religion*, of man's religious consciousness.

27

In our time, clearly, there is a considerable revival of interest in the para-normal, the supernatural, the metaphysical, and the occult, and there is a revival in religious experiments of all kinds. I personally doubt whether this interest in religion as a phenomenon is going to lead towards belief in God. It is, in fact, easy to be 'religious', and many people are finding that they need some such religious 'compensation' for the preoccupations of contemporary secular existence in a technocratic society: Harvey Cox's *Seduction of the Spirit* is a fair description of the whole phenomenon. But I doubt whether these things will necessitate or make more possible men's speaking about God. Even if only because they do not constitute a sufficiently radical questioning of man's basic self-centredness (desire for a balanced life!), the new 'seductions of the spirit' will not bring people back into the world of God of which the Bible speaks, and of which, at its best, the Christian tradition has never lost sight. The possibility of God therefore is more likely to be held open by those who are committed to the way of Christian discipleship in experimental forms, of which the Community house mini-Church is clearly one.

Edward Kessler will tell of what he sees as a direct parallel between 'little people' seeking to tell their story in the face of monolithic city planning, and the disciple-group in the New Testament. Ed Kessler has concluded elsewhere:

> 'In the Gospel stories about Jesus and his group of disciples we find self-authenticating statements about community and prophetic statements about the world. But these statements were made by and about the outsider and the outcast, the last, and the lost.'[7]

I believe that this, again, gives rise to the possibility of God. In the past, it has been assumed by dedicated Christians in churches and in public life that we needed to get decision-making right 'at the top', and thus that we needed to have our disciples in the most influential positions. But the gospel itself had always been in some tension with this apparently wise procedure. In our time, we are seeing the emergence of the small group as the truly prophetic element in society and the place, moreover, where society itself can experiment with attitudes and values into which society as a whole cannot itself venture, at least initially. The God of the Bible is the God who 'pours scorn upon the wisdom of the wise'. 'The foolishness of God' is reputedly stronger than man. Jesus promised 'that the first will be last, and the last will be first'. What happens to a sovereign, all-wise, all-living omnipotent God in this process has always been something of a problem.

What now emerges as a real possibility is that the God who is the

God of the outsider, the outcast, the last, and the lost, may come into his own. God as an additional sanction for those already in authority has begun to appear more and more in our time as a complete racket. Those in authority do not need God, for they have power anyway. If God has any power, it plainly must be different from the power of the powerful. Therefore, the movement of persons from amongst the last and the lost can ultimately only be a movement which raises again the question whether there might not be an utimate reversal of all things, a final way in which power is attributed to the powerless, and a final way in which power is taken from the powerful. Such actions are the actions of the biblical God, dramatized in the incarnation.

Therefore, again, the possibility of God in the present and the future is served, not by those who hang on to the trappings of an authority-figure who in the heavens reflects the big man in the city hall or the government office, but rather upon the little man acting as if he was God despite all the evidence, and claiming the future for himself.

A strategy for the Christian communities of our time obviously emerges even from these two simple examples. We must forbear the temptation to speak more of it here. It has been sufficient to indicate two simple ways in which, as it seems to me, the possibility of God is emerging in the faith-life of some people of our time. In the first instance, an overt bid is made by people to operate the Gospel story themselves. In the second case, the actions of others, both Christians and non-Christians, are seen as part of or as comparable to the Gospel story.

5. Possibility as God

It is perhaps, finally, worth pressing, in an experimental way, the usefulness of leaving the concept of God to emerge under the guise of Future Possibility. In our case, this means a future possibility based upon a concentration of attention solely upon Jesus, and a future possibility based upon the evidence of Jesus-style existence. But there are many other ways of looking at the matter, and it may be salutary to consider some of them.

Almost all contemporary theology has assumed that it was possible and legitimate to use the name of 'God' to describe elements which were more or less foreign to the contexts within which the word was first used. Only with difficulty or considerable subtlety could Paul Tillich's 'Ground of Being', or A. N. Whitehead's 'Process' be identified with the God of the Hebrews or of traditional, much less New

Testament, Christian Faith. And if Black Theology's 'Liberation God' and Ruben Alves 'Freedom God' are nearer to it, they are only so because they have taken one part of the action biblically represented by God, and made it decisive.

Moreover, in the search for what can be meant by 'God', the elements of the unknown, or of futurity, or of eschatology or even apocalyptic have come to play increasingly important roles. Teilhard de Chardin's 'Omega Point', John B. Cobb's 'Emergent Being', Jürgen Moltmann's 'God as Eschatology', Ernst Bloch's 'God as Futurity', or even John Wren Lewis's 'God as Probability', at least have this in common—that they set the reality to which the word 'God' points in the future rather than the past.

The Future as such has, it must be confessed, sometimes been an easy way out of the problem of finding any place within *contemporary* existence for the notion of God. As I have argued, the notion of God cannot survive indefinitely in a situation in which fewer people are in fact using that notion to describe the elements in their existence which have Christian or ultimate significance for them. And, as I have also argued, the actual fact of various people using the name of Jesus (or of God) in relation to their contemporary experience will constitute at least some new data in the modern situation, which is bound to be, as it should be, determinative for future theology. But this is very different from the *avoidance* of the present in some 'theologies of the future'.

However, having said this, the future at least, presumably, means something new. The force of contemporary Jesus-existence, at a time when the images of God from the past are found to be more and more inadequate or impossible, might yet be found to be the persistent insistence upon 'possibility' in the human drama. If the Christians have to live for a time with a more attenuated or a more universal faith (whichever way you look at it), then the fact, or person, or image of 'God' can only emerge in terms not of the past, or of the present, but of the future. The future cannot itself be God, as some of the 'Theology of the Future' asserts. That is to make the past meaningless, and the past is important for Christians, for it contains the decisive Jesus story. It is also to make the present meaningless, and the present is the only possible testing-ground for future possibilities, in conceptuality or in action. Yet the future is the place of possibility. And the constant and recurring reappearance of new possibility might be the way in which God or gods reappear.

For Jesus demands, and Jesus-faith makes possible, God as future possibility, God as the awaited, the unexpected, the emerging, the coming-to-life, the presence as yet but hinted at, the history only beginning to be written, the 'God and Father' only conceivable after man's atheism. 'God' might be what is meant by 'keeping the door of the future open', 'living as if there was more to be revealed', 'awaiting in commitment the conceptuality to confirm that commitment'. Such expectation in the midst of faithfulness, and such faithfulness in expectation, may in the end not be too much unlike the New Testament 'Faith in things not yet seen'. If it does not give one a firm place to stand, it gives one a road to keep walking.

Notes

1. Cf. John J. Vincent, *Secular Christ* (London: Lutterworth Press; New York: Abingdon Press 1968), for all this paragraph. Also 'Christians and the Old Testament', *Epworth Review*, III.2 (May 1976), for that special problem.
2. Harvey G. Cox, *The Secular City* (London: SCM Press 1965), *The Feast of Fools* (Cambridge, Mass.: Harvard University Press 1969); *The Seduction of the Spirit* (New York: Simon and Schuster 1973).
3. John Hick, *God and the Universe of Faiths* (London: Macmillan 1973), pp. 93 f.
4. Maurice F. Wiles, 'Religious Authority and Divine Action', *Religious Studies* 7.1 (1971), 1–12, p. 11. Cf. his *The Remaking of Christian Doctrine* (London: SCM Press 1974).
5. John J. Vincent, *The Jesus Thing* (London: Epworth Press; New York: Abingdon Press 1973).
6. John J. Vincent, *Alternative Church* (Belfast: Christian Journals Ltd; Valley Forge, Pennsylvania: Judson Press 1976); also my paper 'The Para Church: an Affirmation of New Testament Theologies', *Study Encounter* 55 (X.1) 1974 (Geneva: World Council of Churches).
7. Edward S. Kessler, 'Planning: A View From Below', *Crucible*, October-November 1974, pp. 170–8, pp. 173–4 (London: Anglican Board of Social Responsibility).

TWO   JOHN D. DAVIES

Faith as Story

I suppose that every pastor has heard people accuse themselves of 'lack of faith'. 'If only I had more faith, I would be less depressed, or I would understand my children, or I would put the world to rights.' 'Faith' has become a particular kind of commodity, and the agents of the Church appear as policemen to check upon people's diligence in acquiring and retaining this commodity.

In some contexts, 'faith' seems to be a new and special outer coating for the cosmos, a cosmetic to improve the appearance of things. This is, literally, very superficial: but as human beings we need to take great care of the superficial. We meet each other in terms of what lies on the surface, and such surfaces are precious. But a deodorant, spiritual or otherwise, can only conceal trouble; it cannot cancel trouble. It cannot 'save'. Faith must be more than a palliative: according to the Christian gospel, faith can save people, not merely enable them to tolerate misfortune.

Or, 'faith' appears as a kind of spiritual athleticism; it is like having an eye for cricket, something which you either have or do not have, due to some kind of accident of birth. But if 'faith' does for adults what cricket can do for adolescents, it is the surest guarantee of apartheid: and that does not sound like the character of the Christian gospel.

Or, 'faith' appears as a kind of spiritual aesthetic; it's something for people who have the taste for it. It is the result of human initiative and selection. 'Worship God on Sunday in the church of your choice,' says the American roadside hoarding. And this has little in common with the Christian vision of divine vocation and initiative.

The trouble with these ideas of faith is not that the definition has been made wrongly but that the attempt to make a definition at all is misleading. The very question 'what is faith?' implies something about faith, that faith is a thing which you can have. It also implies that we are in an area of authoritative definitions.

Something can indeed be said about faith, but not necessarily in this way. The New Testament has a statement in it which begins 'Faith is . . .' (Hebrews 11:1): but this is a mere headline to the list of specimens of faith which follow. These specimens cover a wider range of

33

situation and feeling than is suggested by the headline, which is in fact not inclusive enough in its abstraction to cover the subject matter fully, let alone to serve as a definition. The writer to the Hebrews, indeed, is perhaps the most systematic and theoretical writer in the New Testament. But when he comes to the subject of faith, he abandons the method of speculative logic and piles on model after model to show what faith looks like.

1. Theology and Storytelling

This, I suggest, is characteristic of Biblical theology. It does not 'theologize': it tells stories. Our contemporary theologies, conservative, modern, radical, or whatever, may include all sorts of disagreements of content, but basically they are cast in the same form. They all assume that theology is a cerebral, conceptual, argumentative exercise. Sometimes, indeed, they become very daring and try to make themselves look as 'scientific' as possible, with plenty of analysis and quantification. The implication is that faith, which is a central part of the subject-matter of theology, is primarily a conceptual matter too.

But theology, as we inherit it from our foundation documents, is not this kind of thing at all. It is a response to events: it is pulled into existence by the experience of a story taking place. The one great result of a century of critical scholarship is not that we can evaluate the historicity of documents or put them in order of compilation; it is that we have been made to recognize how every element in the gospels (and in much of the rest of scripture) owes its existence to the needs and pressures within the life-situation of a particular community needing authority for its propaganda, resources for its apologetic, motivation for its resistance to oppression, and an interpretation of history in a situation of conflict, betrayal, failure, and death. People with this kind of situation are not motivated and upheld by arguments or speculations; they need the emotional and identificational sustenance of specimens, models, paradigms and stories. It is one of the supreme treasures of the Christian inheritance that its fundamental expression it in the form of story and not theorem. Yet so much of our theology, in manner rather than content, seems to reflect a kind of embarrassment about this basic character of the gospel. During times of academic tranquillity, this may not be too dangerous. But I believe that the greatest tragedy exposed by the situation of Southern Africa is the betrayal of the Gospel by generations of Western theological style. All the intellectual competence and academic precision that has gone into making theology what it is today has failed to give the church a strength of soul to expose and to defeat the racialistic myths and misunderstandings of human identity which are destroying the human spirit. Destructive, false and demonic myths are not destroyed by reasoning; they can be conquered by creative, true and healing myths. Critical scholarship has shown this process at work, for instance in the development of the first chapter of Genesis. The battle for the soul needs an armoury of the imagination as well as of the intellect.

It is fashionable at present to be somewhat ashamed of the furore about the 'Death of God'. Indeed, it was a rather unhelpful exercise. It appeared to be the final blow in a competition to see who could be most daring in dispensing with essential symbols. From the situation of South Africa, it looked like a kind of boasting, congenial to people who can play games in a situation of intellectual or cultural security. This kind of theology is useless in a situation where people need renewed and powerful symbols to nerve them to face a situation of oppression. However, the 'Death of God' exercise did catch on, in a way which possibly the theological specialists did not intend. It supplied a headline which at last meant something; it suggested that at last something in theology has actually *happened*. If all that God can do is to die, it is a lot more than he has been allowed to do by academic theology for several generations. At long last, God looked like being, once more, the hero of a *story*.

Elsewhere in our culture, storytelling has its importance. This is particularly noticeable in the educational experience, and not only in arts subjects. Children in junior school start elementary natural science by writing stories of their observation of experiments. Children in infant school are introduced to mathematics by experiencing number, in the form of different lengths of rod, and they see *what happens* when addition or subtraction takes place. We are realizing that we learn from what we enjoy and by events which make an impression. But the 'higher' we go up the education system, the narrower is the sector of the human being that we educate. The primary school teacher addresses the whole child; the university professor addresses a fragment of his student (maybe teachers should be paid according to the percentage of the human being for which they take responsibility). And the study of theology is inevitably bound by extra-strong links to the work-ethic of the last few centuries: learning is work and work is not fun; therefore work which catches the imagination, which appeals to the whole person, is to that extent not work—at least it ought not to receive much academic credit. Learning from concepts and books is easier to control and examine than learning from events, experiences, and encounters. So a pattern of reproductive rather than

35

generative theology is built up, by the whole system of rewards and credits by which the discipline is controlled. And the really disastrous betrayal comes when a student begins to feel that theology does not, and cannot, really *matter* to anyone except within the academic ring. This is a caricature no doubt: the fact that it is a caricature is due to the blessed amateurishness of the best theologians, who have shown that their theology really does matter by the way they theologize off-duty.

Theology is basically about things which happen to people: it is about stories. In this sense it is mythological through and through. Demythologizing is more than just a specialist technique which Bultmann developed for a very special purpose; it is a whole habit of mind which has infested Christian exposition in a context of cultural and intellectual security for many generations. It is a sense of embarrassment at the central element of 'Myth' in the gospel. But the very nature of the Christ-symbol is that Christ is a being who gives meaning to history, in a situation where people believe that history does have a meaning which is not yet fully disclosed. The gospel of Christ, is, therefore, news—good news. It is a story, an event.

If theology is primarily about things that happen to people, this surely must be true concerning 'faith'. If we would catch something of what 'faith' means, perhaps we would do best to stop trying to establish definitions, and instead have a look at some of the specimens or models of faith in the stories of the Gospel. This implies a certain attitude towards authority, a certain understanding of where authority lies. Our culture is a dictionary-producing culture, and this implies certain assumptions about the way meaning is conveyed. But if we assume that the basic key to meaning is not in the authoritative dictionary but in the actual difference that a word makes in the situation in which it is used, we can go out empty, as it were, and discover what a word like 'faith' means from its context. We can try to forget what we ever knew as the supposed meaning of 'faith', and try to see what it is that is present when 'faith' is present. We can try to identify what is being commended when the evangelist states that Jesus remarked on the power of a person's faith, and we can try to identify what is absent when the absence of faith is noted. The chances are that, while these impressions of 'faith' will to some extent overlap, they will not entirely converge; they may indeed apparently contradict each other because of the variety of situations involved.

2. Five Gospel Stories of Faith

1. A paralysed man has four friends (Mark 2:1-12). Jesus is in the

town and there is a crowd around him. He has had the kind of publicity which has made everyone anxious to see him. But the four friends do not join Jesus' congregation; they miss his sermon. They move away from him, and approach him only when they have picked up their paralysed friend on a stretcher. When they get to the meeting-place, they find that the healthy people in the congregation have made Jesus inaccessible. This congregation, wittingly or unwittingly, ensures that the outsider remains an outsider; it is unwilling to make room for an abnormal person to come in. So the four friends do not try to force the outsider in by the same entrance that the ordinary people have used; they make a special way in for him, battering their way in through the roof. They make a hole just big enough to admit the stretcher; then they let the paralysed man down, as if they are lowering a coffin into a grave. And Jesus sees *their* faith, not the faith of the patient. What is faith in this context? It seems to be the insight, boldness and persistence to convert concern into effective action. It is not a 'spiritual' hankering after what you cannot do for yourself: it is a practical insistence on doing the maximum that you can do. It is a refusal to be less than the whole person that you can be. The religious people around take the first opportunity to get involved in a theological argument about blasphemy. The opposite of faith is a preference for non-committal talk rather than active care. Faithlessness does not involve you in knocking holes in people's ceilings. Faith sometimes does. But it also means letting people down and handing over responsibility for them. Faith, in this sense, does not heal: it brings people within range of healing. Faith enables a person to support another person without infringing his freedom.

2. Ten men move around together in a group, bound together by the fact that they all suffer from a skin-disease which excludes them from ordinary society (Luke 17:11-19). They call on Jesus to help them, and he tells them to go to the public health officials and get a clearance to enable them to take up a normal existence. Off they go, and nine of them do exactly what they have been told to do; they continue their urgent journey to the health office—relieved of the embarrassment of having with them a man who could not accompany them into ordinary society, because of his racial classification. This one man detaches himself and comes to meet Jesus and thanks him. In one sense, he has got less to be thankful for than the other nine, because he is still going to be disadvantaged. Jesus notes that it is this underprivileged ten per cent that sees the real point of what has happened, and he says, 'Your faith has saved you'. What is 'faith' here? It is an ability to distinguish the urgent from the important; it is the insight to see that a personal meeting is more valuable than

getting to one's destination in as short a time as possible: faith means leaving the busy road of those who trust in the passports to society given by the guardians of tradition, and joining a man who has no guarantees except himself; faith means deserting the kinds of status given by bureaucracy or public opinion and finding status from one who welcomes the outcast; faith means responding to the overwhelming pressure to be thankful, come what may: faith means to realize that you are loved, that you are not merely a fortuitous beneficiary of a lucky accident.

3. Another outsider seeks help from Jesus, a Gentile woman who wants her daughter cured (Matthew 15: 22–8). She comes crying and wailing, humiliating herself, calling on him in terms of his racial and religious status, emphasizing all the time the difference between himself and herself. She is regarding him as a supernatural magician, and as long as she does so he cannot help her, for this is incompatible with faith. To give her a chance to discover a more human attitude, he speaks to her in as discouraging way as possible: 'It is wrong to take bread from the children and throw it to the dogs.' With some people, this kind of answer would lead to even more violent pleading and self-abasement, or to violent hostility and protest. But the effect on this woman is that she is liberated to discover that Jesus is neither an enemy nor a magician, but a man with whom she can dare to argue and disagree. She answers in effect: 'The difference between children and dogs isn't as great as all that; the dogs always get a share of the children's food, they are part of the same household.' Jesus commends her 'faith'; and she gets exactly the same answer to her request as if she had belonged to the community of the 'children'. What is 'faith' here? It is the exact opposite of a superstitious respect for authority. It is the opposite of a suspension of the powers of reason and discourse. It is seeing the truth about oneself, that the accidents of birth, inheritance and cultural identity are less important than the fact that you are face to face with another person. It is a confidence in your own status as a child of God, and a refusal to accept the depreciated self which your culture insists is the truth about you.

4. Centurions are a curiously attractive class of people in the New Testament. Several times they appear as people of perception and faith, who support the members of the infant church in the face of both heathen and Jewish hostility. And yet, as a non-commissioned officer of the alien occupying power, the general stereotype of the centurion in Jewish society must have been that of the typical fascist (or at least Roman) pig. The secret could perhaps be that the centurion, as the middle-class person sandwiched awkwardly and self-

consciously between the aristocracy and the proletariat, had an instinctive understanding of Jesus' handling of authority. In particular, one centurion has the faith to approach Jesus and seek help on behalf of his boy lying at home paralysed (Matthew 8:5–13). He recognizes that Jesus is not going to be limited by the boundaries of race or culture, just as he has not been limited by the ceremonial laws which forbade him to touch a leper. The centurion testifies to the kind of authority which he sees in Jesus; he is trained to be sensitive to authority, for he is under authority himself and yet also exercises it. He can see that there is one kind of authority, which a privileged man claims because of his birth and inherited status, which he uses to support the system which gives him that status: and there is another kind of authority which belongs to a man in terms of the function by which he serves society. He is surrounded by specimens of the first kind of authority, in both Roman and Jewish hierarchies. But he sees in Jesus the second kind of authority, and this he is prepared to trust. Jesus identifies this as 'faith'. He says that he has never met faith like this, certainly not in Israel, the traditional community of faith. Those who put faith in their inherited status will find themselves thrown out, and their place will be taken by people who belong to God's kingdom not because of automatic membership but because they recognize the subtle, caring kind of authority which Jesus exercises.

5. An example of the absence of faith (Mark 6:1–6). Jesus goes to his home town, where everyone knows him. They are puzzled by the things which he says and does, and ask, 'Where does he get it all from?' 'We know this man, we know his mother and brothers and sister.' And Jesus is frustrated by his lack of faith; he can get nothing done there. What is the 'faith' which is missing? It is not a superstitious regard for some occult force: it is a right understanding of a person's freedom. Unbelief is present when people claim to *know* someone, when they see him *only* as the child of his parents, the product of his ancestry or group or background. Those who have no faith refuse to see that a man can be more than a predictable being, a responder to stimuli, a stereotype. 'Faith', therefore, is a willingness to be surprised, a willingness to find the unexpected in someone whom we think we know. And this is often most difficult in respect of our own family and close friends.

These stories are models of what faith looks like, specimens of faith made visible. They are not moral examples of how to behave. Faith is not a moral virtue, an ability to do good things, so much as something which happens to you. I wish to beware of generalizations at this point; generalizations give us the highest common factor, whereas

39

the fascination of faith is its variousness and diversity. But, if a generalization is allowable, faith appears to be not something which you have but a willingness not to have, a willingness to be surprised, a willingness to have your categories disturbed. It means openness to new possibilities. In this sense, it is rightly and very closely related to repentance.

3. Abraham as Model of Faith

Perhaps the best argument for identifying faith as story, rather than as argument or speculation, is that this is how the New Testament writers themselves identified faith. They were prepared to be more theoretical on matters like the nature of the church or of justification; but in giving an account of the nature of faith they relied primarily on a story. The story on which they fastened was the story of Abraham.

Abraham was the man of faith who went out not knowing; he based his identity not on the known homeland from which he took his origin but on the unknown homeland to which he was journeying (Hebrews 11: 8–10). 'Abraham put his faith in God, and this faith was counted to him as righteousness.' Both Paul and James quote the story of Abraham as the model of faith (Galatians 3:5–9. James 2:18–24). They do so in slightly different contexts, and some interpreters have supposed that there is a radical difference of understanding between the two writers. But let us see what they are each trying to say, not in terms of abstract argument but in terms of the use they make of the story.

James is concerned to insist that faith is no mere intellectual attitude; nor, for that matter, is it a purely spiritual attitude, like 'commitment to Jesus Christ'. Abraham's faith is notable because it was visible in an action, an event. He offered his son Isaac as a sacrifice. He was willing not to have. He was willing not to have his most precious possession, the irreplaceable gift which he had received by promise in his wife's old age. He was willing not merely not to have his son; he was willing not to have the only means by which the earlier promise could be fulfilled, the promise that through his descendants all the world would find its blessing. He was willing to live without a visible future. So he was willing to offer Isaac. It was by the event, not by the mental processes lying behind the event, that Abraham's place in the fulfilment of God's purposes was established; he was justified by his action, by his not-having. This is James' point.

Some people claim that Paul is arguing just the opposite, that it is faith alone, not actions, that justify. But this is to miss the whole story-situation underlying Paul's argument. The opposite of faith, for Paul, is not action but law. 'When God gives you the Spirit and works miracles among you,' Paul asks, 'why is this? Is it because you keep the law, or is it because you have faith in the Gospel message? Look at Abraham: he put his faith in God, and that faith was counted to him as righteousness.'

Paul did not have to be persuaded that faith operates in action. The whole point of his argument in Galatians, the whole living situation which lies behind his letter, is that the apostle Peter's lack of faith was visible in a refusal to take action, a refusal to eat with Gentiles. Obedience to what Peter thought was 'law' led him to fail in action and to break fellowship. Peter's lack of faith is known not because he made some sort of public confession, not because some meter was available for measuring spiritual potential, but because of an uneaten piece of bread and a cold chair on a certain day at Antioch. This is what made Paul furious, an active breach of fellowship, not a spiritual mistake. Peter was wanting, for excellent reasons, to stay within a cultural tabu. In order to retain his relationship with other people for whom that tabu was important, he felt it necessary to be bound by it. And his compromise infected others. It infected the good man Barnabas; friendliness and tolerance were not strong enough resources to defeat a massive and subtle attack on the very heart of faith. The awkward, uncongenial, embarrassing personality of Paul was needed to make a frontal, public, head-on collision with an evil which threatened the central character of the gospel of Jesus Christ. Paul insisted that the disciple of Jesus must be motivated not by a law which frustrates the action of fellowship but by faith which enables the action of fellowship. Like Abraham, the disciple of Christ has a faith which enables him not to insist on retaining the identities and securities which derive from the past, or which depend on the maintenance of a minority privilege. The fact that the Son of God loved *me* and gave himself up for *me* gives me a faith which makes these other securities quite unnecessary. I can live in terms of this faith which links me with all those for whom Christ died, instead of living in terms of a law which separates me from most of the rest of mankind.

Let us return to James. James says that faith must be shown in action. But the very action which he quotes as an example shows plainly that he is not suggesting an action according to a systematic law. James knew as well as Paul that the law of Moses did not exist in Abraham's time. What is more, you cannot legislate Abraham's specific action: you cannot make a law requiring Abraham's action to be performed by all citizens, because Abraham's sacrifice depended entirely on the unique promises and gift that had been made to him. Abraham was saying, as it were, by his action, 'Isaac is not *my* treasure, *my* only son, *my* hope. Isaac is still God's, for God to do with as he will. God has the future in his hand, and I can still go out from here not knowing where I am going.' This attitude cannot be legislated: it is clearly the opposite to the attitude of Peter's dependence on law. Law cannot command faith, or command the works of faith. Law cannot enforce love or integration, but it can forbid them. The separatist laws in South Africa, for instance, in many cases do not need to be replaced by better laws; they merely need abolition. Law cannot force Peter to eat with Gentiles: but the law which prohibits Peter from eating with Gentiles can be removed. It is just possible that faith-like or love-like activities could be compelled by some sort of police-system: it is just possible that Abraham-like activities could be stimulated by some pressures of moral suasion or spiritual bribery or by the offer of some reward. But these would not be the kind of righteousness that derives from faith: and James agrees with Paul that faith is counted as righteousness; he does not argue that righteousness is a substitute for faith.

Paul is able to take the Abraham-story a stage further in raising the urgent question, 'Who are the descendants, the inheritors, of Abraham?' The very willingness of Abraham to sacrifice his only son shows that physical inheritance cannot be all-important, and that another principle may take priority. Does this inheritance, then, consist of those who keep the 'law', those who stick within the norms of a certain culture-group? But this law or culture did not include Abraham himself, so it will hardly do as a definition. No, the characteristic feature of Abraham was this 'faith'. If you want to identify the descendants and inheritors of Abraham, you need to look for the 'men of faith'. Paul does not say 'people with faith in Jesus Christ'— which would again exclude Abraham himself. He does not even say 'people with faith in God', because this would divert attention from the attitude of faith to the object of faith, and there can be sound and unsound kinds of 'faith in God'. Paul literally says, 'those out of faith', those who start from faith, those for whom faith is not an extra piece of clothing or equipment but those for whom faith is the propellant or point of departure. All over the world, in every culture, there are Abrahamic people, people who are willing to risk, to be surprised, to live without guarantees, to enter situations content not to know everything in advance. These are the children of Abraham, because what was truest about him is truest about them.

4. Who are the People of Faith?

This may seem to be far too vague an idea of faith, to people who value the specific character of Christian faith. But this meaning of faith, and only this meaning of faith, needs no redefining when we move to the more precise term 'faith in Christ'. Faith in Christ, the faith commended in the Gospels, is faith of this kind, and it is a kind of faith which is not limited to one linguistic or culture group, or even to one kind of psychological type. Nor is it limited to the obviously 'free' people: it can include people who, by accidents of history or circumstance, happen to live lives which some would consider to be very law-bound, highly structured, or systematic. There are many deeply free and faith-ful people to be found among orthodox Jews, members of religious orders, lawyers and engineers. By contrast there are faith-less people who make a ritual of their freedom from ritual, or who justify themselves in terms of a past decision to be free which is receding ever more distant from the present and becoming an ancient emblem. Faith, to judge from the specimens in the Bible, has little to do with a person's cultural inheritance. Faithful people are able to live within a system without being in bondage to it. This is, after all, what we are doing with language all the time; we are using the system of language and would be unintelligible if we did not do so: yet we are continually creative within that system, because we are continually saying things which neither we nor our associates have ever said before.

So there are people of faith everywhere. The specific power of the Christian gospel is that it gives a story to this faith, a story which fulfils and acts out this faith, giving it human substance and history while not distorting the basic attitude called 'faith'. It supplies a mythology without which faith might be only a shapeless yearning: it supplies a community, without which faith is hindered in growing into the action of fellowship.

The action of the story of the Gospel enables faith to be. Paul is enabled to shake his fist in Peter's face and to point to the cold chair and the uneaten bread, not just because of 'faith' in the general sense, but because of 'faith in the Son of God who loved me and gave himself for me'. Ultimately, it is this personal passion, motivated by something which has happened and which matters, which has nerved people to do and to be beyond all expectations. It is this which has sometimes brought strangely-assorted, rather conservative, Christians together on the firing-line, while their more articulate and more sophisticated colleagues have found reason conveniently to be elsewhere. The earnest, conscientious, well-educated, English, liberal

Christian has built into him at every joint a friction pad that makes it virtually impossible for him to move with enthusiasm. Enthusiasm, partisanship, commitment to a cause, all seem to be incompatible with the balanced medium-ness which is what we call respect for truth. Tolerance is mildly amused by enthusiasm, and insists that it be kept for peripheral activities like golf. And indeed, the violence of some other countries with big cities makes English tolerance seem a precious blessing. But tolerance assumes that enthusiasm must be partial and therefore a deviation from truth. Oppressed or defeated peoples cannot afford the luxury of this kind of tolerance, and develop instant or lasting mythologies. It may be that the English are a very privileged and unusual people in this respect: the last war that was fought on their territory was between two groups which no longer have any real identity, and that was 300 years ago; and they have found reason to export their men of violence to contribute to a history of fighting on other people's territories. But communities which do not have this kind of privilege find it difficult to apprehend truth which is expressed only in propositions and generalizations. Truth which is expressed in generalizations is no match for the mythologies in terms of motivational effect. Faith as proposition is relatively powerless: faith as story can meet our mythologies on their own ground, as mythologies, and can confront a partial or sectional enthusiasm with a critical, saving, universal enthusiasm.

The story-form in which gospel has come to us can therefore overcome the righteous anxiety of the earnest good man; it can cut through the apparent incompatibility between truth and enthusiasm. In our own day, particularly, it seems that the story of Jesus is being claimed as the most enduring, vigorous, and adaptable story in our culture. Bach's and Pasolini's interpretations of Matthew continue to attract people. The L.P. of 'Jesus Christ Superstar' is one of the best sellers in the world. I think, in fact, that the Jesus-myth is taken for something of a ride in 'Superstar', but that does not alter the point. I see the real hero of the show as Judas; the pressures brought on him by authority, his vulnerability as a black man in a white world, the agonies which surround his fulfilment of the role of informer, are the most subtle parts of an otherwise unsubtle show. And the Jesus-figure is best understood as the Jesus who exists in the shifting fantasies of Judas. Jesus the plastic godbox superstar and Jesus the maudlin overwashed hippie make sense as characters in Judas' bad dreams, but not otherwise. The point is that the Jesus-story can stand up to this treatment and not be damaged. Or consider 'Godspell'. 'Godspell' could never have happened before; it had to wait for an extraordinary combination of cultural factors to converge. But it has suddenly disclosed, as never before, the character of the learning-situation of the disciple-group around Jesus. It gives a window into the educational laboratory set up by Jesus; its insight is compatible with the gospels, but has been hidden from us by centuries of authoritarian assumptions concerning the manner in which learning takes place. One is left amazed at the variety of perceptions which are latent, waiting still for discovery, in the faith-story of Jesus. Could anyone credibly apply the 'Godspell' approach to the myths of Prometheus or Hamlet?

5. Story as Creator of Future Faith

In conclusion, if faith is known in story, what does this have to say to church, as agent and communicator of this gospel? Briefly, there seem to be three specific forms of activity which belong to the Biblical communities and which implement the idea of faith as something which happens to people.

1. The prophets *taught by doing things as well as by saying things.* Jesus picked up this tradition and used it, for instance, in the very activity which he devised for his friends as the means by which he should be remembered, the means by which his membership with them should be renewed. There is a specific skill of devising events or 'happenings' which will educate at a point where lectures, sermons, and discussions cannot reach. If it is to be true to the manner, as well as to the content of the Gospel, the church needs to ensure that it educates with events like this. It needs to recognize and develop methods of education which depend on intuition as well as intellect.

2. 'Godspell' reminded us at several points of the process by which the parables of Jesus came into being: someone comes along with a story or an idea or a situation, and someone else is able to see another slant on it, to turn it around and make it personal, or to see all sorts of connections which are not obvious at first sight. *The parable develops both creativity and freedom*: it encourages people to look on the creation and on life around them with an eye of imagination and humour. It also leaves the hearer free to understand or to refuse to understand: it enables the hearer to contribute to the learning process, so that what he learns is his and not something which continues to depend on the teacher. Jesus' parable-style teaching was an implementation of his concern that ultimately the distance between teacher and pupil would be abolished. The teaching church needs to gain skill and sensitivity in the use of parables. And, if it is to engage in real conflict with demonic mythologies, it will need

consecrated imaginations as well as consecrated intellects. For this, parables are an obvious training-ground.

3. The most urgent mandate to church, however, is surely to *enable God's story to continue to happen in the world*. The gospel of Jesus Christ is more than an inspiring idea or an educational programme. It is the story of a new power breaking into history, the story of a unique confrontation and defeat of the powers of evil. The New Testament is the story and the evidence of the effect of Christ on people, not only through the activities of Jesus of Nazareth but through the community of faith which derived from his activities. People were healed, people were fed, people were reconciled, people were opened to the truth about themselves and about each other. Authorities, stereotypes and mythologies were upset, and demons cast out. The Kingdom of God was brought near, with a new set of priorities and commitments. A team of people went into action as agents of historical change. They did not set up a programme for their own survival, either as individuals or as church, for their whole idea of faith enabled them to live without a visible future; they were able to leave the issue in the hands of God, and got on with the job of exposing and attacking evil in the present situation. Where they went, miracles happened: God acted, not to make the church more impressive but to make people whole. This is how faith was transformed into story; later, men came along with their words and pens, and put the story into the form in which we have received it. But the writing always comes after the happening.

One day, someone may be able to write down the story of how faith happened amid the disorders and despairs of our contemporary society. But, before the story can be told, it must be acted: and that is the activity of faith. Our task is to get on with making the story.

THREE   EDWARD S. KESSLER

A Jubilee and Disciples

In this paper, we will concentrate on the ministry of Jesus, on the stories of that one to three years in which he moved about, in or near the land of his people.

We will experiment. We will argue as if the stories of Jesus and the patterns that appear were still decisive and possible for the ministry of Jesus' followers in this age. Incidentally, we will argue that they should have been at other times.

We are not forgetting what came after the ministry. We are not reducing the importance of the crucifixion, the resurrection, the coming of the spirit or the development of the Church and its tradition. What we want to say is that these other main elements of Christian thought need constantly to be re-interpreted in the light of new information and new understandings of the living Jesus and the time he spent with his friends and his enemies.

In the main, we shall take the record as it stands. I do in fact believe that most of the particular sayings we shall study can be demonstrated to be authentic to Jesus, at least in major part. By concentrating on one gospel—that of Luke—I do not intend to avoid critical questions, but rather to show how certain major 'lines' appear, lines which clearly were important to some early Christians, whose Jesus was the hero behind them (whether or not historically they are 'genuine').

In the first section of the paper, we will talk about two central themes of Jesus' ministry, justice and the development of a community. We shall suggest different understandings of justice and community from the usual, progressive, socially-conscious lines of thought.

1. Jesus 'avoids the Issues'

What the Jesus-centred person wants to do is this: try to discover what the words and actions of Jesus meant to the people of his time, in order to discover what sense they could make of Jesus, in terms of the questions in everyone's minds. We would by no means argue that the only questions of his time had to do with 'revolution', 'freedom', 'liberation from the enemy army of occupation', and the like, but we know that such questions burned fiercely in the Jewish consciousness and exploded in violent revolt about thirty-five years after Jesus' death. .

Let us take the only story from Jesus' ministry which appears in all four gospels, 'The Feeding of the Five Thousand'. Focusing on the story of the desert meal, we will perform a do-it-yourself analysis which, while not dealing with a multitude of detailed, academic or scholarly questions, may yet lead us to certain conclusions, conversions and even actions.[1]

First, re-read the four tellings of the story of the feeding of the 5,000 men (only Matthew adds that there were women and children in addition to the 5,000 men), as in Matthew 14:15–21; Mark 6:34–44; Luke 9:12–17; John 6:3–15.

Second, place yourself in the position of a Roman official, especially one concerned with keeping a watching brief on revolutionary or potentially dangerous movements. Write your own report about this desert meal, based on information received. Include the following 'facts':

1. Jesus is a wandering, radical prophetic figure about whom some extreme claims are being made;
2. Jesus has designated twelve of his followers as a special inner group—the twelve being an obvious reference to the twelve tribes of ancient memory, but with radical implications for the present;
3. Jesus' twelve include one known revolutionary (Simon the Zealot), one possible assassin (Judas Sicarius?), and other dangerous types such as the 'Sons of Thunder', alias James and John, sons of Zebedee;
4. Tax collectors, important figures in the Roman administration, are beginning to gather to him, and at least one has 'changed sides';
5. Jesus was brought up in a town in an area of the country known to be a hot-bed of revolutionary zeal, and probably has personal connections with many wanted criminals and insurgents.
6. The gathering of 5,000 men in a desert place can only be regarded as extremely dangerous to political stability;
7. Whilst the man Jesus does not seem willing at the moment to assume leadership of any revolutionary movement, there

appears to be a growing demand to place him at the head of
the movement;

8. Certain revolutionary views have been expressed by the man
   Jesus, such as 'prisoners will be freed', 'poor shall inherit the
   earth', and the like;

9. Jesus' followers claim to be non-military and non-violent, yet
   the feeding of the 5,000 men was conducted according to
   military drill, with the men seated in ranks of 50s and 100s:
   a definite military flavour; and, finally,

10. Jesus was reported to be sorry for the 5,000, 'because they were
    as sheep not having a shepherd'. This innocent-sounding
    phrase has for the Jews military meaning.

The wildest sort of tensions and the most extreme expectations ran
side by side through the society of Jesus' time, as they so often do in a
country occupied by a military conqueror. The alternatives were clear
in this situation of absolute opposites: either you went along with the
situation, co-operating with the rulers as did the High Priests, the
Sadducees or the tax-collectors; or, you proposed radical changes and
took the necessary military measures to carry them out. So, from
our experience of occupied Europe under the Nazis would we understand the choices.

But Jesus refuses to accept these choices; he refuses to affirm the
Roman rule, and he refuses to lift the sword of rebellion. The poor
shall be lifted up, the mighty thrown down, the captives freed—but
not by the sword. That which is insignificant shall become significant;
that which is nothing shall become something; he who is no one shall
become some one. He shall be some one who is able to love his
enemies, the Roman soldiers who could make him walk a mile, or
hand over his best overcoat—some one who can walk an extra mile
with his oppressor or hand over his jacket as well as his overcoat.

'If you can't beat 'em, join 'em' is an American political motto, to
which might be added, 'but whatever you do, don't try to fight them
unless you mean to try to win!' But to Jesus, obviously, a victory won
by overpowering your oppressor or opponent is the kind of victory
you can win only by doing a deal with the devil, the one who can
place in your hands all the kingdoms of the world (Luke 4: 6). The
victory of the Kingdom can only be won when men take responsibility for their actions, and when they act in love rather than under
the domination of the powers that be above them. Such a victory is
worth dying for.

But, for the practical world, this message is no use. It simply does
not face the issues: for those in authority, the issue is to keep the

situation as steady as possible; and, for those who recognize their oppression, the issue is to determine how and when to strike at the oppressor.

Of course, one may argue that there are other possibilities. In times of trouble, most people will just try to stay out of sight, to stay out of trouble. Alternatively, if you think God is not well served by what is going on in your world, you may join a community and retreat into the wilderness to await whatever it is that God will produce to change the situation. But these alternatives Jesus does not seem to have considered. You cannot change the world either by accepting and affirming it, or by simply renouncing and avoiding it.

2. The Real Issue: A Jubilee

A. *Proclaiming the 'Jubilee'*

Is Enoch Powell right in saying that Jesus (and therefore Christianity) has nothing to do with politics? Is it enough to quote, as Powell does, 'My Kingdom is not of this world'? The only way to deal with such entrenched establishment attitudes is to set forth what Jesus stated as a practical, worldly programme and then see if in the gospels and in the later church anything happens which might have resulted from such a programme.

At the beginning of his ministry, Jesus came to his home town, Nazareth, and, in the synagogue on the Sabbath day, read 'the lesson' as follows:

'The spirit of the Lord has been given to me,
for he has anointed me.
He has sent me to bring the good news to the poor,
to proclaim liberty to captives
and to the blind new sight,
to set the downtrodden free,
to proclaim the Lord's year of favour'

(Luke 4 : 18–19, *Jerusalem Bible*)
(from Isaiah 61 : 1–2).

Then, in what has been described as the shortest and best sermon ever preached, Jesus says, 'This text is being fulfilled today even as you listen' (v. 21).

It seems to be agreed that 'the Lord's year of favour' (or, in the older translations, 'the acceptable year of the Lord') is an unmistakable reference to the Jubilee Year. To understand what the Jubilee is, we have to fly backwards to that little-known Old Testament book, Leviticus, and turn to chapter 25.

We all know vaguely about the Sabbath idea. Not only were the people supposed to rest on the seventh day, but in the seventh year as well. In the Sabbath year, the seventh, farming was to cease, and the people were to trust that God would provide a sufficiently bountiful harvest from the sixth year to carry them over until the eighth year. Then, after seven sabbaths of years (forty-nine years):

'... in the day of atonement shall ye send abroad the trumpet throughout all your land. And ye shall hallow the fiftieth year, and proclaim liberty throughout the land unto all the inhabitants thereof; it shall be a Jubilee unto you; and ye shall return every man unto his possession, and ye shall return every man unto his family...' (Leviticus 25:9–10, Revised Version).

God had decreed that no Israelite should be a slave. If a man in financial trouble had to sell himself for his debts, he might become an indentured servant—but only until the Jubilee:

'... then shall he go out from thee, he and his children with him, and shall return unto his own family, and unto the possession of his fathers shall he return. For they are my servants which I brought forth out of the land of Egypt: they shall not be sold as bondmen' (Leviticus 25:41–2).

We do not need to decide whether the Jubilee was practised in ancient Israel, never, seldom, often, or unfailingly. What we need to see is that Jesus spoke publicly in an imagery that had clear and practical consequences in the minds of his followers and of all the people who heard him. However difficult it might be to work out the details of a Jubilee; however little the rich establishment might like the idea; however unrealistic or naïve the demand for a Jubilee celebration might seem; nevertheless, the Jubilee is a down-to-earth, here-and-now, this life, solid suggestion, proposal or programme.

Nothing in the gospels opposes Jubilee; many stories, parables and sayings pick up the Jubilee theme one way or another. Re-read the story of Zaccheus (Luke 19:1–9). Zaccheus is a wealthy senior tax-collector. When people complained that Jesus had gone to a sinner's house,

'... Zaccheus stood his ground and said to the Lord, "Look, sir, I am going to give half my property to the poor, and if I have cheated anybody I will pay him back four times the amount..."' (Luke 19:8).

To put it in other words than those of morality and repentance, Zaccheus pledges himself to put the Jubilee into practice. Another most interesting example of the use of the Jubilee theme is contained in that mysterious parable in Luke 16: 1–8 of the unfaithful steward who adjusted everyone's debts. The crafty steward's 'astuteness' is surely because he has put the Jubilee into practice to save his own skin.

B. *Building a Group Of Disciples*

You cannot mention the word *group* today without people thinking either that you are involved with a Pop Group or that you are into group dynamics. Yet we need the word 'group' or something like it when we come to talk about the disciples. We have too long gone up the cul-de-sac of individual discipleship. We have moved so far away from the original concept of Jesus, as it was developed in the early Church, that nowadays if you tell most Christians that they cannot really be Christians without being in some form of group, they are really quite horrified. 'I should have thought', these English Christians might say, 'that being a Christian has to do with prayer, worship and personal behaviour.'

Yet a substantial part of Jesus' ministry was unquestionably dedicated to the building of a disciple group. And that group, I suggest, was always intended to be the 'model' for the Church. The easiest and best evidence for this intentional model is (*a*) the survival of the original group of disciples (less the one traitor), and (*b*) the spread of the Church around the Mediterranean coasts on the 'cellular' principle. Mission through the multiplication of 'cells' (which some now think is 'way out' Christianity) was not just a convenience; nor was it just the only workable option. The struggles in the early Church were not whether there ought to be groups of Christians meeting in small numbers in each place, but how to keep Jesus at the centre of each group.

Jesus built up his disciple group or cell by internal disciplines. 'First shall be last', 'Leader shall be servant', 'Love your enemies' and 'Take up your cross' are obvious examples. We will pick up some of these themes in a later section on Church Strategy. For the present, we will look at the key elements in starting and maintaining a dedicated, world-changing group in a time of stress and distress.

3. Rewards in the Life of the Disciple Group

The beginnings of the creation of the disciple group occur right at the beginning of Jesus' ministry, with the call of the first disciples, the fishermen Simon and Andrew, and then James and John. Denis Potter, in his television play *Son of Man* is one of the few modern people who get the joke. When his Jesus delivers the famous line, 'I will make you fishers of men', it is given with a laugh, the kind of laugh that recognizes the utter foolishness of the idea that the Kingdom of God will come into the world through them, the kind of laugh that could be shared by a group of friends who know that they are nothing, who suddenly begin to talk about how great they are (Matthew 4:19; Mark 1:17; Luke 5:10–11).

Luke's gospel tells the story of the formation and development of the disciple group in a series of narratives whose sequence can be taken seriously from the point of view of typology, if not also historicity. After the temptation by the devil in the wilderness, Jesus begins to teach in the local synagogues of his home territory (Luke 4:15). There he creates a general mind-blowing freak-out not only by announcing his purposes (give good news to the poor, proclaim liberty to the captives, set the down-trodden free, announce the Jubilee year) but immediately *refuses* to give those signs of power that might convince the local people. He goes too far. He reminds them that in a famine Elijah only fed a widow who was a foreigner living in a foreign city; Elisha only healed one leper, who was Naaman, the Syrian! So salvation is not for those who expect to be rewarded by God. Salvation is for those who do not really know that it is even in the neighbourhood (Luke 4:16–30).

Jesus then teaches 'with authority' in Capernaum, though his only recorded 'teaching' consists in casting out a demon from a possessed man. Then he goes to Simon's house and heals his mother-in-law of a fever—which may be a way of telling us that Jesus knew Simon before he called him to be a disciple. Then, after a series of healings, Jesus leaves Capernaum to travel through Judea, and it is only then Luke tells us of the call of the first four disciples—Simon and his partners James and John Zebedee—after the miraculous catch of fish. So, getting in on discipleship starts with sudden riches—and a vision so powerful that the riches can be dropped along with the fishing nets (Luke 5:1–11). Let us look at the rewards promised in Luke's gospel.

REWARDS

After the call of the first four disciples, we get a series of stories telling about the immediate rewards in the life of the disciple group:

1. *Parties:* Levi, the tax collector, called to be a disciple by Jesus, immediately gives a great party for Jesus and his friends (Luke 5:29).

2. *Eating and Drinking:* As opposed to the disciples of John the Baptizing one and the disciples of the Pharisees, Jesus' disciples are not always fasting and saying prayers, 'but . . . go on eating and drinking' (Luke 5:33).

3. *Breaking old rules:* Jesus' disciples don't have to keep the old rules—they walk through the cornfields picking the ears of corn, rubbing them in their hands and eating them *on the sabbath* (Luke 6:1–5). Commentators, following Luke's text, make much of the violation of the Sabbath regulations, but I am tempted to think less of the Sabbath regulations than of children stealing apples from someone's orchard—as David had taken the bread from the house of God.

4. *The 'nobodies' who follow Jesus will get the highest honours:* Jesus deliberately chooses twelve apostles (Luke 6:12–16) and later tells them, 'You will sit on thrones to judge the 12 tribes of Israel' (Luke 22:30).

5. *Jesus' disciples will get back more than they have to give up:* 'Give, and there will be gifts for you: a full measure, pressed down, shaken together, and running over will be poured into your lap . . .' (Luke 6:38).

6. *A disciple is on solid ground:* A true disciple, says Jesus, is like the man who lays the foundations of his house on rocks (Luke 6:46–9).

7. *A disciple gets to hear the real thing:* 'The mysteries of the Kingdom of God are revealed to you; for the rest there are only parables . . .' (Luke 8:9–10).

8. *The disciples are the true family:* Jesus said, 'My mother and my brothers are those who hear the word of God and put it into practice' (Luke 8:21).

9. *Disciples gain their lives:* '. . . anyone who loses his life for my sake, that man will save it' (Luke 9:24b).

10. *Disciples get to see the real thing:* 'Master, it is wonderful for us to be here . . .' cries Peter at the transfiguration. See also the 'Johannine thunderbolt' (Luke 10:17–24).

11. *Disciples stand in for God:* To his disciples, Jesus says, 'Anyone who rejects you, rejects me, and those who reject me reject the one who sent me' (Luke 10:16).

12. *A true disciple does not always have to 'produce':* Martha and Mary in Luke 10:38–42.

13. *Disciples will be given what they need to eat and drink:* 'Set your hearts on his kingdom, and these . . . things will be given you as well' (Luke 12:30–1).

14. *Disciples will be rewarded for their sacrifices now:* When Peter says, 'What about us? We left all we had to follow you,' Jesus says: 'I tell you solemnly, there is no one who has left house, wife, brothers, parents or children for the sake of the kingdom of God who will not be given repayment many times over in this present time and, in the world to come, eternal life' (Luke 18:28–30).

15. *The despised events carried out by nobodies will judge the rest:* Perhaps the greatest reward of discipleship is that what the disciples have been and done with Jesus, and what they will yet do in his name will stand in judgement of the world. If you cannot see the humour in such an idea, then you have been going to church too long. (Being too serious and solemn and long-faced?) The judgement is to be made by those who love their enemies and rejoice in that loving.

We have gone on at length, picking out only the fifteen most obvious statements of immediate rewards for the disciples. Naturally, we must go on and look at some of the risks as well. However, here is a mass of evidence in one Synoptic Gospel about immediate joy, pleasure, gratification and reward. The hard bits are never to be taken without the lovely stuff in mind! When, in our careful and cautious way, we hear Jesus say, 'I am telling you not to worry about your life and what you are to eat, nor about your body and how you are to clothe it' (Luke 12:22), we run for cover. We think of sound reasons why we must go on 'planning ahead', we prove that Jesus didn't really mean it, certainly not for our situation. Instead, we should rejoice that discipleship means an end to such cares. We do not need to affirm all layabouts or drop-outs who live off the work of others; we need to see in our own time those who are really the fishing net-droppers: 'There is no need to be afraid, little flock, for it has pleased your Father to give you the kingdom', says Jesus (Luke 12:32).

4. Risks in discipleship

We do not use words like 'risk' and 'reward' lightly. Partly, we are concerned with reversing a traditional Christian emphasis, and correcting the *order* in which we speak of risks first and rewards second. The common feeling about much Christianity is that if you make big 'sacrifices', here and now, you receive an ultimate 'pay-off'. We read the gospels in the reverse order. Jesus seems to be saying to his followers that they will have plenty of joy—earthly fun—but there is a grave risk—in fact, there are several risks. One risk in the gospels is the cross; another is what people will think (you must be mad, a fool, etc.).

Many professing Christians will refer to the cross in their own lives, the cross as a living experience. Very often, this cross will turn out to be some personal suffering—the death of someone dear, or a painful affliction they have to suffer. They will look to Jesus, especially to the cross, to help them in their suffering. With great bravery and patience, they will say, 'We have to bear these crosses'.

The trouble with this kind of popular Christianity is that this sort of suffering and the courage it sometimes calls forth has almost nothing to do with the cross in the gospels. Put it this way: there are three kinds of suffering, and a variety of responses to them, thus:

SUFFERING	ORDINARY RESPONSE	'CHRISTIAN' RESPONSE
Deserved suffering, e.g., punishment for wrongdoing	Avoid it; hide out; curse if you are caught	Repentance; sorrow for other sufferers who do not really deserve it
'Random' suffering: accident or painful disease	Other people may say that you *must* have done something to deserve it	To offer love, healing, forgiveness, acceptance
Suffering for doing what is *right*	Others will say you are doing what is wrong; you will say 'It's unfair'.	Rejoice in yourselves; forgive those who cause you the suffering.

A recent writer has well said:

> 'The believer's cross is no longer any and every kind of suffering, sickness, or tension, the bearing of which is demanded ... It is not, like sickness or catastrophe, an inexplicable, unpredictable suffering; it is the end of a path freely chosen after counting the cost ... it is the social reality of representing in an unwilling world the Order to come.'[2]

The words of Jesus predicting his crucifixion are usually dealt with in one of two ways. Traditional interpreters see in Jesus' predictions evidence that he foresaw God's great plan to have his Son take the sins of the world on himself: the cross, then, is the known end of a

56

great divine pageant. Radical biblical critics have been inclined to think that Jesus never really spoke words predicting his 'Passion', but that they appear in the gospels because the early Church read them back into the events. On the latter view, the early Christians argued: if it happened, it must have been foreordained, it must have been part of the 'Plan' of salvation, and Jesus must have known it.

In reality, there is a sensible alternative way to read not only Jesus' predictions of his own crucifixion but also his clear statements about the cross to the disciples:

'If any man comes to me without hating his father, mother, wife, children, brothers, sisters, yes and his own life too, he cannot be my disciple. Anyone who does not carry his cross and come after me cannot be my disciple' (Luke 14:26–7).

We can read these as statements of unavoidable *risk* rather than as prediction of events to come. Once again, as in the case of the Desert Meal, it is John's Gospel which gives a clue. In chapter 21, the resurrected Jesus speaks to Peter about his fate in poetic language, indicating

'... the kind of death by which Peter would give glory to God. After this he said "Follow me".

'Peter turned and saw the disciple Jesus loved following them... Peter said to Jesus, "What about him, Lord?" Jesus answered, "If I want him to stay behind until I come, what does it matter to you? You are to follow me." '

So John is not less a disciple for not having been crucified. He took the risk with the rest. The risk is inescapable; the result is not for us to determine.

What does the life of cross-bearing discipleship mean today? It would merely arouse the comment, 'Don't be a damned fool'. To undertake a discipled life, to choose a voluntary, nomadic poverty in order to be along-side the far too numerous poor of this land would be something only a fool would do. The establishment wouldn't think of you as a criminal so much as a damned nuisance, particularly if you are someone of education or breeding who really has the choices of this world before him.

The response of the people of Jesus' time is more violent, but the questions put to him are similar:

Who do you think you are? 'They said, "This is Joseph's son, surely?"... But he replied... "....no prophet is ever accepted in his own country" ' (Luke 4:23–4).

Even your family knows you've gone round the bend. '... his relatives . . . set out to take charge of him, convinced he was out of his mind' (Mark 3 : 21).

So you think you're so clever . . . 'Play the Prophet', said the Sanhedrin guards to the blindfolded Jesus; 'Who hit you then?' (Luke 22 : 64).

So you think you're so powerful . . . 'If you are the King of the Jews, save yourself' (Luke 23 : 37). 'Are you not the Christ? Save us and yourself as well' (Luke 23 : 39).

The 'straight' and steady people of his day recognized Jesus for the dangerous simpleton that he was: too simple really to understand the 'problems' of the day; very dangerous to those in the seats of authority. But even Jesus recognized the truth about his own selected disciples when he said, 'I bless you, Father, Lord of heaven and earth, for hiding these things from the learned and the clever and revealing them to mere children' (Luke 10 : 21).

What a thing to be a disciple! Not only does the 'world' get angry and call you stupid for going off on a nonsense 'mission' when there is 'real work' to be done, but even the master you follow calls you children!

5. Theological Training for Disciples

The wholesale criticism of the disciples by Jesus as recorded in Mark is toned down in Luke. But there too, we find ample evidence that what appears to be the training of the disciple group by Jesus, in fact does not appear to have been conducted with great psychological sensitivity. Either that or the disciples were chosen for their ineptness. Or maybe discipleship was not based on agreement and comprehension, but on obedience and apprenticeship.

The Disciples are mentally slow: Jesus has patiently to explain parables to them so that they may understand. Luke 8 : 9. They are described as reacting to Jesus' words: 'But they could make nothing of this; what he said was quite obscure to them, they had no idea what it meant'. (Luke 18 : 34).

The Disciples are weak in Faith: Jesus says, 'Where is your faith?' (Luke 8 : 25). 'Give them something to eat yourselves', (Luke 9 : 13). 'I tell you, not even in Israel have I found faith like this' (Luke 7 : 9).

The Disciples would like to keep it all for themselves: John spoke up 'Master,' he said 'we saw a man casting out devils in your name, and because he is not with us we tried to stop him' (Luke 9 : 49). 'People even brought little children to him, for him to touch them; but when the disciples saw this they turned them away' (Luke 18 : 15).

A Jubilee and Disciples

Some Disciples had childish ambitions; and they could not stick together when the crunch came. An argument started between them about which of them was the greatest (Luke 9:46 and 22:24). 'Why are you asleep?' he said to them. 'Get up and pray not to be put to the test?' (Luke 22:46).

These are only a few of the evidences for the sort of people involved in the inner ring of disciples. We have mentioned already the tax-collectors who were friends of Jesus as examples of criminal tendencies among the disciples; also we noted hints of his association with political fanatics Simon the Zealot the most obvious, possibly Judas Sicarius (?), or the 'sons of thunder' (Luke 6:13–16 and Mark 3:17–19). Perhaps we should summarize these characteristics or 'qualifications' for the disciples, and couple them with Jesus' methods of training, as if the first disciple group were also the first Jesus-centred theological college!

GOOD NEWS THEOLOGICAL COLLEGE
(one-year or three-year training course?)

Qualifications for entry	Courses	Staff	Practice
Ambitions	Leader as servant	Children	Foot-washing
Lack of perception	The hidden kingdom	Demons Lepers	Healing: staying in people's homes
Swindler	Self-understanding	Widow	Reparation*
Exclusive	Finding the lost	Foreigners	Going outside Galilee
Possessive	Recognition	Competitors	Don't condemn
Violent	Love your enemies	Roman soldiers†	Walk two miles
Quarrelsome	The way	Son of man	Cross-bearing
Weak in faith	Crises	Fig-tree, storm	Walking on water

* or 'give back four times what you stole'
† Part-time staff

59

Students admitted will be expected to bring cloak, staff, sandals (should be strong and in good condition), and empty food basket. Walking, boating, climbing and mountain-moving are major sports. Practical pastoral and mission work emphasized. Fees: all you possess.

How much easier for us in the established or main-line churches of the West if we could only deny the essential truth of this picture of Jesus and his disciples. If we could say that it is all nonsense, we would not have to explain how far we have moved *to the opposite extreme*. The list of the seven qualifications for Jesus' disciples would today be a check list of those characteristics that must be avoided. We have heard of a South American Protestant Church which decided on the ordination of selected lay people, and went into a study of which occupations were likely to produce 'suitable' candidates for the local ministry. Doctors, lawyers, judges, teachers, etc. were obviously acceptable. The line was finally drawn just above carpenters. They were obviously unsuitable.

The churches mostly live as if Jesus had got it wrong, as if only the wise, the influential, the well-to-do could understand the foolishness, the weakness, the poverty of God. Yet if we take such a view, by what we say or by the way we minister, we will get little sympathy from Paul, who understood perfectly that he must repeat the same wrong moves that Jesus made in the selection and training of his disciples. To the Church at Corinth, Paul wrote:

'Take yourselves for instance, brothers, at the time when you were called: how many of you were wise in the ordinary sense of the word, how many were influential people, or came from noble families? No, it was to shame the wise that God chose what is foolish by human reckoning, and to shame what is strong that he chose what is weak by human reckoning; those whom the world thinks common and contemptible are the ones that God has chosen —those who are nothing at all to show up those who are everything' (1 Corinthians 1:26–8).

We have attempted a partial and one-sided statement of Jesus' ministry. We have not tried to argue that our statement represents the whole gospel. But we do suggest that our practical view of Jesus' ministry adds up to four 'lines' which can be taken seriously. Put in summary terms, they add up to a *fourfold way or technique*:

1. Do not accept the questions as the world put them, nor feel you have to choose among alternatives defined by the world;

2. Put the Jubilee into practice;
3. Form disciple groups, which put into practice the liberation and discipline of the Kingdom of God and obey the Jubilee ordinance;
4. Provide training for the disciple groups.

So far, what we have written is 'only' theology. We need now to test some of the ideas from Jesus' ministry against real situations in our churches and our world.

6. In the Church

At a recent meeting of a diocesan pastoral committee, a request was received from a certain parish we shall call 'Town', a market/industrial town parish of about 20,000 population. 'Town' includes an area known as 'Southtown', a new, lower working-class estate of about 4,000 population about to have more houses built in it after a hiatus of some years. The parish has a second church—a twenty-year-old dual-purpose building—in Southtown. There is little Southtown support for the church, though a considerable amount of youth work goes on in the dual-purpose building.

In the end, the Pastoral Committee was very discouraging about the possibility of further support, partly on the justifiable ground that the parish of Town had always had two curates and should work the matter out internally. What the parish of Town wanted was support for an additional worker to concentrate on Southtown, and support for the dual-purpose building.

The conclusion may have been inevitable, given the church's limited and dwindling resources of manpower and money, but the discussion was revealing. After it had been stated that the Methodists had had to withdraw their man from Southtown, a member of the Pastoral Committee who was familiar with the Town situation remarked that one had to understand that Southtown is a 'missionary area'. Questioning revealed that 'missionary area' meant a lower working-class area from which few people would support the church. 'So,' added another member, 'you can tell that it is a "missionary area" by the fact that the Methodists have withdrawn their minister, the Church of England won't support an additional worker, and the community-serving building may have to be closed for lack of support!'

The whole situation is a comment on the perilous state of the churches. Those in authority think that the churches are in peril because of the shortage of money, manpower and support and instinctively judge situations of local churches by their economic prospects, and the 'strength' of their congregations. The gospel, however, takes a different view.

1. *What are the Real Issues?*

We need to analyse that unfortunately typical situation from the gospel's viewpoint. We need to say that just to do something 'in the name of the church' is not a standard; what we do as 'church' must be under the judgement of the standards of Jesus' ministry. A practical Jesus-centred view might raise such a question as:

Resource distribution. Those in authority are right to put the question to the local churches: 'Are you practising the Jubilee in your own church? If the "poor" are in need in your place, you must not expect outsiders to make up for what you refuse to do in your own church!' Equally, those in the local church are right to say to those in authority above them: 'You must practise the Jubilee with the resources you have inherited and divert support from the better-off places to the poorer ones. You dare not use worldly economic standards as the major basis for distributing the church's wealth.'

The practical implications of a gospel view of resource distribution are enormous. Take the situation in the Church of England. Until very recently, almost all the clergy were paid by the dead (endowments). One might with profit make a penitential study of where the money came from originally, how it was assumed, and how many poor people had to suffer in ancient times so that the Church might prosper. But let us remain in the present. The Church with its money has two choices in gospel terms which are never considered: one is to give it all away; and the other is to see that the income is dedicated entirely to work with the poor. The 'give it all away' alternative cannot be considered because it would not be good stewardship: we cannot have faith in God to provide ministry for his Church (we prefer faith in sound business management).

The idea that all *endowment* income should go to support mission among the poor is equally intolerable to the powers-that-be in the church. A barrage of questions and counter arguments are thrown up, such as:

(a) *'We have a mission to all the people.'* The argument comes quite naturally to the Church of England by law established. But the gospel does *not* allow us to consider that the mission to the rich is the same as the mission to the poor; that the mission to the lost, the outcast, the sick is the same as the mission to those who have it good, to those who are doing well, to those who are well.

(b) *'Who is really poor?'* Many in the churches think that by asking this question (which has some merit), they can justify any sort of ministry, even one that is distinctly biased towards the suburbs of this land, and, indeed, the suburbs of the world. Every country has its rich and poor, it is true. But whether the majority are really poor (as in a poor country) or whether only a minority is really poor (as in England), the Good News is still for the poor. The poor are not hard to find in the inner cities, among the immigrants, the old, the young—in fact everywhere except among the enclaves of the rich. Ministry to the richer people is a vital part of the ministry of the gospel, but it must have a gospel-shape. Here are some observations the rich do *not* usually make:

(i) *The rich have less need of traditional ministries.* If the suburban churches want to maintain a traditional church life, they are far better staffed with lay people who have the traditional qualifications to preach, teach, evangelize, visit, organize, finance, etc.

(ii) *Ministry to the rich is a call that they give themselves in service to the poor.* To be fair, many well-to-do people suspect the system which has produced their privileged position because of accidents of birth. They suspect the suburban gospel. In the Church, we cannot criticize our suburbanites without offering them the same challenge that Jesus offered the rich young men—the chance to shed his inherited privileges, to join the disciple group with its risks and rewards and disciplines, to make a new start.

2. *A New Ministry: the Disciple Group*

Even if the churches made the decision to live by the style and content of Jesus' ministry, that decision would not be the actual start of the journey, the new start of the gospel. To decide to re-shape and re-form its ministry would be an act of penitence for the churches, an admission that what we do now is actually moving away from the gospel.

The new start for the churches will be the development of a new style of ministry; a style much nearer to that of the first disciples:

—we must give up trying to do things *for* the poor (or, more likely, doing things *to* the poor);

—we must open our resources to being used by the poor as they decide they should be used—not as we think best for them;

—if the poor of the inner cities and such places are to continue to suffer, then we must find ways to be alongside them, exposed to the same suffering;

—if there is not enough money to keep open both poor and rich churches, to keep the plant going in the inner city as well as in the suburbs, then the rich, suburban churches will have to be closed; and, above all,

—new institutions must be created which enable real meeting to occur between rich and poor, on the home ground of the poor, and in their style and language.

Many Christians will struggle to understand the meaning of all this. They will think that all that it means is that dear old St Dives' Church in the Suburbs must be closed, and they must drag themselves into the dilapidated St Lazarus by the Gasometer for the Sunday morning service. It would be little use, because St Lazarus Church itself is peopled with commuters, who used to be of the inner city and are no longer so. Anyway, the St Lazarus' people will tell you how they tried to have a youth club, but the little vandals made a mess of their newly-painted hall, and the club had to be stopped.

The difficulties of creating new institutions, a New Model Church, will be enormous; if we try to build on the base of the old model, the difficulties may be insuperable.

3. *New Model: the Church of the Jubilee.*

People do not always appreciate the difference between 'practical' and 'politic'. It goes without saying that our proposals are not 'politic', that is, they will not be approved by the powers-that-be nor accepted by many in the local churches. 'Practical' is something else—it should mean something that could be put into practice. Jesus defined practical ministry for us, put it into practice, and made his followers carry it on and extend it. If today's churches seem to have moved very far from the substance, style and model of Jesus' ministry, then we need to begin to be the 'practical' men and women who do the 'politic' thing before God, and make a new start.

4. *Theological Re-training*

We cannot begin here to talk of the detailed planning, re-planning and re-training that would be required even to begin to convert today's churches into the model of the ministry of Jesus. What we can say is that we have begun to restate and to re-emphasize the nature of the person on whom we mean to base our claim to be God's people. If we preached such a gospel in our churches, we would have to live by it. If we once decided to live by such a gospel, the changes would come thick and fast.[3]

7. In the World

The question about being a Christian in the world is one that is taken seriously by all Christians, however much their answers may vary. One interesting view is that there is a higher discipline for professing Christians to take on themselves, though we can accept a lower standard for non-church people. A simple case in point would be that of divorce where the churches (mostly) were saying in effect, Christian marriages cannot or should not end in divorce, but we do not oppose the existence of secular divorce procedures. In fact, some church bodies, recognizing the serious pastoral problems created by marriages breaking up, have produced enlightened and useful studies on marriage.

Some rigorists might argue that Jesus' rules on ethical matters apply to everyone. People shy away from such positions because they seem old-fashioned and, perhaps more importantly, because they raise the old ghost of using the power of the state to enforce certain moral standards. So the churches sometimes seem to say 'We will keep a higher rule, God's law, for ourselves, but we will not attempt to enforce such rules on a no-longer-Christian population'. To some, this will sound as if the churches are becoming 'sects', trying to live a pure life in an impure world, but letting the world get on with its orgy of self-destruction.

However, what seems clear to us from our study of Jesus' ministry are the following points:

1. Jesus meant his 'rules' to apply to everyone: Roman officials, soldiers, Sadduccees, Pharisees, prostitutes, criminals, ordinary people;
2. Jesus was determined not to use force;
3. Obedience to Jesus' 'rules' had to be voluntary;
4. Obedience to Jesus' 'rules' meant a great upheaval in the way things were generally done (what we like to call 'the system').

To round off this essay, let us take one modern situation, that of Town Planning, and subject it to the test of the lines of Jesus' ministry.

TOWN PLANNING

The modern world is slightly less blinded by science than it was a few decades ago. Certain lessons are being learned the hard way, mostly that 'scientists' who help make public policy gave the answers and then framed the questions to fit the answers.

As an alternative approach, we will apply to Planning the lines of Jesus' ministry as we have described them:

1. Facing the issues;
2. The Real issues: proclaiming the Jubilee;
3. Building a group of disciples:
   Rewards, Risks and Disciplines;
4. Providing alternative Training.

1. *Facing the 'issues'*. Planners face the issues that they have the scope and skill to deal with. Planners' issues come under such now traditional headings as 'land use' or 'traffic'. When dealing with traffic it is not surprising that planners have focused on 'congestion' or 'traffic jams' or 'delays'. Congestion is a visible problem, annoying in that it impedes the way things are done, being especially irritating to the rich and powerful. Congestion can be cured (it used to be thought) by building more roads, especially urban motorways. Then, somehow, more and more people and more and more local authorities began to recognize the disaster course on which we have been set. Cities have been ripped apart, homes destroyed, businesses dislocated, air fouled, neighbourhoods made unliveable—but the 'problem' was not 'solved'. Congestion of traffic increased until the Arab oil sheikhs intervened.

2. *The real issue was proclaiming a 'traffic jubilee'*. It was that the blind should walk in safety, that the old and infirm should move about freely and easily, that traffic planning should be good news to the poor, those too young to drive, the car-less. Typical traffic planning to produce a paradise for the motorist was turning out to be the exact opposite of the Kingdom. The more you do for the motorist, the slower and less frequently the buses of the poor run, the worse off is the mother and her children in the New Town or on the new estate. We avoided the real moral issues of first and last; by putting the first first, we were leading to the destruction of all. When, in the future, people walk or ride their bicycles over ruins of once-great highways, what will they make of us? They will not mind our foolishness if we repented in time and declared a traffic Jubilee, with less emphasis on 'efficiency' and far more on justice. We look on in amazement as motorway plans are cut back or cancelled or politically defeated in many places; even more, funds are made available for planning bicycle trails through the cities. Parable? Sign of the times? Repentance? Time will tell.

3. *Building a group of disciples*. Planning is an idealistic profession, and many planners hold high ideals about their part in helping people and improving the world, or at least a small part of it. However, there are many ordinary people, especially those threatened or actually harmed by 'planning' who will suspect that planners will not make

ideal disciple material. Yet the clear lesson of Jesus' ministry in the selection of disciples is that there are no 'ideal' disciples, just people. Some are called, some not; some respond, some turn away, and no disciple group seems complete without potential traitors or trouble-makers in its midst.

For planners to be converted in order to come into some form of disciple group, they will have to put away any vestige of the old arrogant approach of knowing what is best and doing good things for people whether they like it or not. They will have to find ways to be among those they serve, to learn to listen to and hear what people are really saying about their lives, and to work to make planning in practice far more responsive to those they might unintentionally oppress.[4]

The *rewards* of planning with people and in response to them can be great. One reward is the feeling of excitement in the sharing of a new kind of 'mission'. Another reward is the fellowship of those who are also in on the 'secret'. Above all, there is the reward of making new friends of the poor with whom this planning Jubilee is to be shared.

The *risks* are great as well. The great movie man, Sam Goldwyn, is reported to have said, 'I don't want a lot of yes-men around me. I want someone who will stand up to me and say, "No!"—even if it costs him his job!' Some planners of the Jubilee may have to face such risks. More often, the risk will be more painful: being ridiculed and ignored more or less simultaneously. Your report disappears into the files of limbo. Your suggestions are dismissed out of hand. Promotion comes slowly if at all. You are definitely not 'in'.

The *discipline* of a group of disciple planners, though voluntary, will have to be strong enough not only to meet sudden crises but to endure through long periods of little or no visible progress. In a way, planners are well suited to such disciplines because of the nature of their profession, because of the long time it takes to make a plan and the even longer time it takes for anything to result from the plan. The same waiting discipline will now need to be applied in the expecta-tion of a new thing happening.

4. *Providing Alternative Training.* The *training* of planners for membership of disciple groups will mean re-training for most planners and re-training of a kind not really available in any existing institu-tion. A new sort of 'radical' or 'alternative' Town Planning Institute needs to be established in which can be encouraged the formation, maintenance and training of disciple groups of planners. New kinds of expectations from groups and people must be made, beginning with members of the planning profession. Many of us see that for

practical and moral reasons we are coming to the end of the era of industrial growth, economic development, and hoping that if we make the rich richer, somehow the poor will get a bit better. We still have a little time, considerable resources and lots of talent to make friends by using our power and resources.

The Kingdom Is Breaking In, And The Jubilee Has Been Declared To Begin On The .... Day Of The .... Month Of The Year .... Let Each Man Declare The Time For Himself.

Notes

1. Some of the following is based on Alan Dale's work with U.T.U. in a Study Week on St Mark, in December 1974. See his *New World* (Oxford University Press 1967) p. 6. On what follows above, see in general John H. Yoder, *The Politics of Jesus* (Grand Rapids: Eerdmans 1972). Yoder reviews the earlier discussions including those of S. G. F. Brandon, which he modifies.
2. John H. Yoder, *The Politics of Jesus*, p. 97.
3. For a start, see: *Ministry in Cities* (Sheffield: Urban Theology Unit, 1972); *Ministry Between Yesterday and Tomorrow, New City*, 7/8 (1974); *Doing Theology in the City, New City*, 11 (1976).
4. See the reports and essays of planners and theologians in *South Yorkshire in Search of a Soul, New City*, 10 (1975).

FOUR   ROY B. CROWDER

Inner City Incarnation

1. A Piece of Incarnation

In late summer 1971, six of us moved into a large old house
in Pitsmoor, Sheffield. We had decided to form a Christian community
in an inner city area. It started as a temporary experimental situation.
The area into which we moved was subject to comprehensive redevelopment plans and our house was only expected to exist for
another eight years.

Two things motivated us, mainly. First, we were concerned to create
a community. Some had lived in community already, others had
sought it in some form for a time, the rest had a feeling it was right.
Secondly, we were anxious to live and minister in an inner city area.
We felt that Christian witness that said nothing to or about the
material and social conditions of people's lives was an empty vessel.
To outsiders certainly, though not always to those who are resident,
Pitsmoor has all the characteristics of an area of deprivation. There
is plenty of bad housing; there are plenty of bad landlords—and the
most difficult to budge is probably the Corporation. There are high-
rise flats and new estates, replacing the old back-to-backs with impersonal maisonettes; redevelopment has moved many younger
people out and greatly dislocated the old structures of community;
there is quite a large immigrant population of mainly West Indian
origin; there are few facilities for the young in terms of play space,
or youth clubs or schools with a vigorous life in the locality, and the
teachers live on the other side of the city; old people get isolated,
middle-aged people have their energy sapped by living amongst
demolition sites for years on end; 'problem families' seem to be moved
in as a Corporation policy and become scapegoats for the local
residents who can cope; while for people who pass through the area
by bus or car the 'blacks' or the 'scroungers' are the scapegoats;
lastly the churches are poor and ailing and their most competent
sons and daughters have gone or will soon go.

As we moved into the house we had with us certain assumptions.
We were looking for ways of living together which would be mutually
supportive, for that sense of community which we thought was a

69

prerequisite of the body of Christ.[1] One of the most important elements of this was economic sharing, and from the start we arranged a system by which residents paid a proportion of their wages into a common pool. This means that those with secure, stable and professional jobs pay significantly more than those doing part-time jobs. At the start this meant that one of the members who did not earn enough to live on was supported and able to work energetically in the neighbourhood, forming a youth club and working closely with a neighbourhood action group. Again we were anxious that nobody fell into restricting roles in the house. Cooking and other forms of work about the house are shared. It is often fascinating how people ask the female residents whether they do all the cooking!

We were also looking for ways of embodying in action the whole ministry—the life, as well as the death and resurrection—of Jesus: and not just one part of it. Our main assumption about the task of being a Christian community in a locality was expressed in the phrase: the area writes the agenda. We considered this to be a proper response to the incarnation—Christ becoming human, the Divine taking on the limitations of humanity. Incarnation suggests that anyone seeking to minister in a deprived area should at least make the commitment of living there and becoming part of the neighbourhood, listening carefully and avoiding as many preconceptions as possible. The area is the agenda—what else could be? The first task, then, is to find out what is going on and to begin to be accepted.

Two elements were specially significant in our coming together— dissatisfaction with current forms, and hopes for a new way of life. They are, in fact, central in the community movement as a whole in this time of social unrest. In his book, *Communes in Britain*, Andrew Rigby comments on exactly the same elements in otherwise varied communal experiments. He offers a useful understanding of the growth of communes in contemporary society of which we are a part.

Arguing that to understand the growth of the movement, you have to discuss 'the particular life problems encountered by members of particular social groups located in particular areas of the social structure', Rigby describes two main factors. The first is *the question of identity*.

> 'Thus, it is a common observation that the bulk of the commune membership is made up of young people drawn mainly from middle class social backgrounds. It can be argued that what has rendered increasing numbers of middle class youth available for recruitment to the commune movement has been what many people have termed the problem of personal identity. . . . What seems to have happened

as a consequence of the forces of urbanisation, industrialisation, bureaucratisation and the centralisation of decision-making is that the power of such public institutions as the factory and the work place and the national polity over the individual has grown at the cost of those institutions concerned with the private areas of life (e.g. family, local community, and religion). It can be argued that the operations of such public institutions are increasingly dominated by norms and standards that are rational only in terms of the operation of the institution as a whole. Little concern is paid to the individual caught up in such organisations. Within them he has little opportunity to develop a meaningful sense of his own worth. He is treated more like the proverbial cog in the machine than an autonomous, thinking, conscious human being.'[2]

For middle class young people in particular, who have been brought up to consider themselves worthy of respect, and to think that their work might have some value, this view of society is repugnant. Far from accepting that one's personal worth can be estimated in terms of material goods possessed, some seek a more personal, mutual, co-operative and intimate network of social relationships, than seems possible outside.

The second factor Rigby describes as *the breakdown of institutional hypocrisy*, which occurs in a time of rapid social change.

'That is, every society is characterised by a discrepancy between the actual everyday practices of its members and the dominant ideals to which lip-service is piously paid by these same members. There develops a common-sense stock of knowledge about when and where it is "reasonable" to expect people to adhere strictly to certain central values, such as "Thou shalt not kill", and when and where it is "unreasonable" to hold such expectations, such as in times of war. Young members of society are expected to become familiar with and to internalise such examples of the taken-for-granted hypocrisy of everyday life. However, in times of rapid social change this institutionalisation of hypocrisy can break down. New situations and practices emerge, with the result that the areas of "value-exemption" have not had time to be defined and generally accepted. The universal gap between principle and practice appears with unusual clarity at such times, particularly to the young who have to some extent been shielded from this phenomenon within the confines of educational institutions where they have been instilled with the dominant values of the society. This perception is one of the most common sources of youthful radicalism, and one

71

of the responses to such experiences is to seek to join or form a commune.'[3]

Not only do these two factors explain much of the background of the general commune movement, they have a particular relevance to Christian communities. The members of our house have all been or still are members of traditional institutional churches. A common observation about mainline churches is that their size, dispersal, and financial complaisance discourage people from risking themselves in a community of sharing, mutual support, or respect for people with different patterns of behaviour. The same dynamic which locates respect for people in their career status or financial security can equally find reason for disrespect in a particular pattern of behaviour. It is not easy to find acceptance in a mainline congregation if you are 'unrespectable' or feckless or delinquent or freaky. It is not surprising that a search for a deeper common life should arise from this situation.

Equally important as an impetus to the young radical Christian's search is the concern about institutional hypocrisy. The gospels if read enough in public worship provide ample evidence of 'dominant ideals to which lip-service is piously paid', while everyday practice is different. The current demand that British churches cannot live off the earnings of apartheid by investing in corporations or banks with direct links with South Africa rests on a classic case of a discrepancy between ideal and practice being accepted because it is far enough away to be conveniently overlooked.

2. Action and Reflection

So much for how we get there in the first place, what happens once we are there? In a community concerned with Action and Reflection, it is not always easy to know which follows which. Indeed, most of the time, actions are both the result and the cause of reflection. Sometimes careful thought about how to proceed has come first, so that we avoid imposing our own unconscious values on a situation we are only beginning to know. People who arrive with a knowledge of what an area needs and who seek to impose that pattern are not responding to the openness and vulnerability of the incarnation. The neighbourhood action group which we helped to start and which has become very strong over the last three and a half years was an example of how we thought it right to proceed. We regarded our role in setting up the group as rather like that of a catalyst.

We discovered that the area was under threat of clearance, but that the Corporation were prepared to consider the idea of making the neighbourhood of some 600 dwellings a General Improvement Area. We invited a small number of local residents we had come to know into our front room and discussed the situation. Most of them were long-term residents; some had been born and brought up in the area and were keenly opposed to, though quite ignorant of, the plans for comprehensive clearance. All the south side of Pitsmoor had been built to accommodate the nineteenth-century workers in the steel-works and on the railway. The smallest dwellings were built at the bottom of the hill and had since been cleared. The better-class houses, originally for managers, doctors, etc., had been built in this higher section and most of them were substantial. A subsequent wave of artisan dwellings meant that some of the houses were too small to be improved or to have indoor plumbing fitted, but the majority could be improved gradually with minimal dislocation of the community.

Out of our initial conversations came the idea of a public meeting. When held, it was attended by more than any local political meeting in the previous few years. A committee was appointed which has since met every month in the community room in our house. Since then members of the house have been members of the committee, but have taken their place as local residents, not as people running a committee for the neighbourhood.

At other times reflection about what has been going on was provoked after the event. On more than one occasion people who have stayed in the house for varying lengths of time described how they found the community life healing, and have showed us in retrospect the potential of the hospitality we simply enjoyed giving. One girl came to stay with us after a particularly difficult time working as a volunteer in a hospital for disturbed children. She came because her close friend was living here, and she liked what she heard of her work on a playbus. On leaving she sent us a card saying: 'with much appreciation for setting me back on my feet after the traumas of High Wick! There's nothing like Ashram atmosphere to provide anyone with a bit of stability and security.'

Stability and security are probably not the first things we would have said about ourselves, and this is not to say that everyone has found healing by living in the community, but merely that you do not always know what you were doing until you get called a neighbour by someone who needed you.

How, then, can reflection on the ministry of Jesus begin to form a framework for Christian action in the community? Does one simply have to muddle along doing what comes naturally? Our experience would suggest that reflection on the figure of Jesus in his ministry

73

has been of central importance to us in our search. For a discussion of what that has meant I would like to focus on the call to discipleship recorded in the third chapter of Mark's gospel:

'He then went up into the hill-country and called the men he wanted; and they went and joined him. He appointed twelve as his companions, whom he would send out to proclaim the Gospel, with a commission to drive out devils.' (Mark 3:13).

The pattern is clear and is the fulcrum for the rest of the gospel. The disciples are called out to be with Jesus; to preach; to heal; to travel with him along his way. Later, after they have been hooked, it is explained that this also means they have to take what comes and keep going:

'Anyone who wishes to be a follower of mine must leave self behind; he must take up his cross, and come with me. Whoever cares for his own safety is lost; but if a man will let himself be lost for my sake and for the Gospel, that man is safe' (Mark 8:34).

Thus, the disciples became part of the gospel story—and this, it seems to me, has been the shape of our involvement. We, like them, have been called to be with Jesus, to proclaim the gospel, to make sick people better, to be prepared for suffering and to follow the way that Jesus goes.

3. Being with Jesus

The disciples are called out. There always seems to be a debate in the Church about how the disciple should be 'in the world but not of it'. Christians were seen in the first centuries as being aliens in their own country. As the letter to Diognetus has it,

'they dwell in their home country, but as if foreigners there. They share all things as citizens, but suffer all things as strangers. Every foreign country is their home country, and every home country is a foreign country' (Ep. Diogn. V. 5–6).

Certainly it is hard to strike a balance. Being an alien can mean pharisaical self-righteousness. Being 'in one's home country' can mean throwing out the Christian baby with the humanist or religious bathwater, and losing the proper scandal of the gospel. Certainly the meaning of this is going to be different for different people at different times. Mainly it is going to depend on what it means to 'be with Jesus'. This is the nub of the response of discipleship.

74

What it means to be with Jesus depends on our image or picture of Jesus. It is precisely this that has been clouded with historical and cultural trappings which need to be pulled away so that the meaning of incarnation in our time and for our time can become clear.

Two of the most resonant pictures of Jesus to be described recently come from Adolf Holl and Roger Garaudy. In his book *Jesus in Bad Company*, Adolf Holl, a German Roman Catholic theologian forbidden to speak by the ecclesiastical authorities, begins to locate Jesus in his own time and society. He argues that those aspects of Jesus' life which stand out to us in our secular age may very well not be the most distinctive qualities which would have spoken to his contemporaries. It was not unusual for a wandering worker of miracles to lead a religious group at that time in the Middle East, but Holl argues there are three, historically attested, peculiar facts about Jesus' relation to the society of his time which may be the start of a new attitude to life appropriate to modern times and conditions. The three are: being a social outsider, ignoring customary kinship hierarchy, and downward social tendency.

> 'What was Jesus' attitude to the society in which he lived? The answer to this question is determined in the first place by the event in Jesus's life that ended it, and that is historically most reliably attested—his execution ... outside the city, in accordance with custom, thus indicating that the delinquent had placed himself outside the accepted order of things. The mere fact of Jesus's execution is sufficient to mark him clearly as a social outsider. This sociological conclusion is supported by two further historical facts that have their roots in Jesus's life and whose influence on the development of Jesus's fate are clearly recognizable. There is the fact of the insignificance of Jesus's own clan when it came to a regulation of the leadership question within the religious movement that gathered momentum after his death, and the fact that Christianity first spread itself in the lower social classes of the then Mediterranean world.'[4]

Many arguments have been put forward to explain Jesus' execution. Either Jewish society was wicked and deliberately did to death the Son of God, or they were sadly mistaken and killed an innocent man. But neither of these arguments is plausible. Jesus was an outsider who refused to conform to the rules of a strictly organized society; he behaved in a criminal manner by putting himself above the law; he deliberately flouted the ruling authorities even using the recruiting slogan of the Zealot revolutionary movement as his own: 'Take up your cross'; he was not a violent, *realpolitik* revolutionary nor a

75

merely reactionary criminal, but he managed to threaten the Roman and Jewish authorities more than either by his claim to make all things new.

> 'His alternative was so relevant, so much a threat, that Pilate could afford to free, in exchange for Jesus, the ordinary Guevara-type insurrectionist Barabbas.'[5]

It is sometimes difficult to imagine how conformist Western Christianity could have metamorphosed from such a beginning. The suffocating respectability of our churches has moved the gospel of Jesus radically from its original position in and around the criminal periphery of society to the centre of that society's precepts and values. Only at occasional times of stress—the Confessing Church in Nazi Germany, conscientious objectors in Second World War Britain, or the anti Vietnam war movement in the States—have significant groups of Christians lived against the state machine. This kind of analysis raises deep questions about the location of the disciple in the 'social geography' of his time—questions which are only compounded by the other two facts to which Holl makes reference.

Holl's second claim is that Jesus was unusual as the leader of a religious movement in neglecting kinship relations in the regulation of the leadership question. Contemporary religious movements recognized membership of the founder's clan as a crucial argument in questions of succession. But for the followers of Jesus this kind of claim never made any headway. Jesus seems to have considered that the relationships of the new community he founded were of more significance than the ties of the kinship bond. Immediately after the call to the disciples which comes in Mark 3 his family come to collect him. They are obviously embarrassed by his behaviour and think he is mad. His reply is clear enough.

> ' "Who is my mother? Who are my brothers?" and looking round at those who were sitting in the circle about him he said "here are my mother and my brothers. Whoever does the will of God is my brother, my sister, my mother" ' (Mark 3:34–5).

Again it is not easy to see how this Jesus has become the image of the family man and the protector of the claustrophobic life of the modern nuclear family. The impetus of his way seems to have been against all the forms of social organization which become a straight-jacket on human relationships. Those bonds which become restrictive on the new community are to be avoided. The important thing is the search for new community across the barriers of family or class or clan.

The third significant element highlighted by Holl is the downward social tendency of the movement Jesus started. His birth did not take place in the royal palace as the wise men expected, nor did his ministry make any impact on the powerful or rich. Indeed, the difficulties rich people would find in following his way are often made plain. The story of the rich young ruler is clear. The people among whom Jesus moved were the poor and outcast. Even the region he came from was out of favour. As Holl says,

'it is not difficult to visualize the constitution of Jesus's first audience: piece-workers, tenant farmers, itinerant shepherds, fishermen, perhaps a few artisans, and some women and children.'6

This is not to mention those tax gatherers and prostitutes outside the moral framework to whom Jesus spoke as one with authority, not as a condescending or self-righteous member of an upper class.

The notion of poverty has always attracted considerable attention as a part of the Christian life, though often a few specialists have been left to get on with it on behalf of the rest. In almost every situation there is a renewed interest in what that might mean for us today. Holl rightly points out that monetary wealth is not the only criterion. Vocabulary or education can equally be a source of wealth and power, even though people are not outrageously rich. Whatever the criteria, it is clear that this presents an enormous challenge to the Church in the Western industrialized nations, which is very near the top of the pile, whatever measure you use. They have little understanding of what it means to be at the bottom of the pile, and even less desire to learn from those who are there. But if we are being called to a life of minimal security, in which the proper social direction is being stood on its head, and careers or possessions or relationships are being called into question, then we cannot escape the challenge of the location of the Christian group in society.

For us, living in a run-down area of a major English city has been an important location. What poverty means in the private affluence and public squalor of modern society is not simple. There are people with high incomes—one of the members of the youth club we ran showed us his pay cheque the other day with more than £70 to show for a week's work—and yet their access to educational opportunity or to power over their own environment is severely restricted. This problem obviously taxes other inner city communities, like the Passionist Mission in Liverpool.

'The poor of society will never know liberation unless they are given power over their own destinies. So often it is a problem of education and the understanding of the ways and means to cope. In working with people and not simply for them, maintaining a deep respect for their personal dignity and privacy, the Mission has attempted to face this deeper problem.

It is so necessary for the Religious Life and the Church to give very prayerful and deep consideration to this life of witness in contemporary society. This it must do not only in the Third World but within the deprived sectors of our contemporary urbanised civilisation. This is an ever present and nagging worry in the prayer and work of this Mission. In such worry and prayer we feel we have come anew to understand the basic spirit and future challenge which our own Religious Order can deepen and face: the meaning of the powerlessness of Jesus in his sufferings and his liberation in his resurrection revealed in the world around us.'[7]

We would tend to agree that the powerlessness of the people who live around here is one of the crucial aspects of their poverty, though one must not discount how many people just do not have enough money to sustain a decent life.

4. Proclaiming the Gospel

So, the call to be with Jesus calls some of us out of secure, middle-class or professional views of how our future ought to be, into an eccentric mixed community, working out any rule it might need as it goes along, in an inner city area of deprivation and dislocation. What then can it mean to preach the good news?

A recent comment on an Anglican clerical deployment Report suggests that this is neither a recent nor an easily tackled problem in an area such as ours:

'The Report suggests that at the present "there are 'unchurched millions' in newly-built areas, in growing towns, and on the outskirts of our cities", and mentions also the deprived inner-city areas with their special human and social problems ... *But that is the way our cities have been since the industrial-urban revolution took hold of our society.*'[8]

Ted Wickham's book *Church and People in an Industrial City* also demonstrates the basic failure of the churches to discover their mission to the industrial working classes of our society since the beginning of the eighteenth century.

'The one (factor) is the continued estrangement of the working classes, still enlarging, more and more colouring the urban and industrial areas, flooding into suburban areas. We have traced it at length, generation by generation, in the City of Sheffield. Their history, in this respect, is one of general continuity of habit, but with the decline of the denominations that had been more effective in reaching the working classes, with the political re-orientation of their leadership, and the solidification of their own pattern of life, and with the general weakening of religious faith in the whole nation, they were even more wholly outside the religious institutions as the twentieth century advanced.'[9]

In this situation, we feel that there is little point in merely talking. People have heard all the words about Christianity that they want, and are still in the majority of cases unconvinced that it is good news. This must not be confused with a rejection of the gospel. We are not the sort of people who would stand on street corners preaching about salvation, or carrying placards, though we are not afraid of standing up in public for beliefs or causes we hold dear. We think that this kind of approach is at best a narrow one, at worst a perversion of the meaning of proclamation. The only clear way the gospel will be bodied forth is in terms of actions in the mundane situations of secular existence, actions which will demonstrate a commitment to a way which transcends in detailed practical matters the ordinary way of living..

Here, our second picture of Jesus drawn by the French Marxist Roger Garaudy puts us on the right lines:

'In the time of the Emperor Tiberius's reign—no one knows exactly when or where—an individual whose name is not known suddenly opened up new horizons to men.

Quite certainly he was neither a philosopher nor a tribune, but he had to live in such a way that his entire life would signify that each one of us can, at any moment, make a new start.

Dozens, perhaps even hundreds, of popular story-tellers have spread abroad the good news. We know three or four of them.

The shock they received was expressed in the images of simple people, of the insulted and the injured, of the sad at heart, when they dream that all things have become possible: the blind who begin to see, the paralyzed who walk for the first time, the hungry in the wilderness who are given bread, the prostitute in whom the woman is awakened, the dead child brought back to life.

So that the good news could be proclaimed to the full, it was necessary for this man to tell the world, through his resurrection, that every frontier, even the ultimate frontier of death itself, had been overcome. Some scholar or other may question every fact of this man's life, but that will alter nothing of this certainty which changes life. A fire has been lit. It bears living witness to the spark or the original flame which gave it birth.

First of all the fire was a rising of the wretched: if this had not been so, the "establishment" from Nero to Diocletian, would not have dealt so hardly with them.

With this man, love had to be militant and subversive: if this had not been so, he, the first, would not have been crucified.

Until then, all the wise men had meditated on destiny, on necessity confused with reason. He showed them their folly. He who was the reverse of destiny, who was liberty, creation, life—he took the inevitability out of history.

He fulfilled the promises of the heroes and martyrs of the great awakening to freedom. Not only the hopes of Isaiah or the wrath of Ezekiel. Prometheus was unbound. Antigone freed from her prison walls. These chains and walls, mythical images of destiny, crumbled to dust before him. All the gods were dead and man began. It was as if man had been born again.

I look upon this cross, symbol of this new birth and I dream of all who have widened the horizons: of St. John of the Cross, who taught us to discover everything by virtue of having nothing, of Karl Marx who showed us how we could change the world, of Van Gogh and of all who made us realize that man is too great to be sufficient unto himself. You, the beneficiaries of the great hope of which Constantine robbed us, men of the church, give him back to us! His life and death belong to us, too, to all for whom that hope has meaning, to all who learned from him that man is created as creator.'[10]

Living 'as if man had been born again', and then swopping stories about it is the only way forward for Christian proclamation now. It is a modest way, but a possible one. For us, it means talking about what we are doing. On many occasions we find ourselves telling visitors what we are here for, and how we see ourselves. Often we are asked by the kids from the youth club or those who come with housing problems, what we are doing and why. For many people in the area the comprehensive term 'students' covers us—despite the fact that we are mid-twenties and earning money. For others we live in 'that house where they help you with the Housing'. For yet others we 'belong' to the church across the road. At least these are realistic appraisals of how we seem to act, and that is a good way to start communication.

It is easy to ignore the widely and deeply held stereotypes and prejudices that people have about words like 'Jesus' or 'Christianity'. Their experiences of school religion, or television religion, or memories of Sunday School, have relegated Christianity to boredom, hypocrisy or respectable niceness. Only personal meeting with people who demonstrate in their lives a commitment to others in the name of Jesus can begin to reclaim the lost ground of centuries.

5. Making Sick People Better

The healing ministry of the Charismatic movement hits the headlines now and again. Many Christians who hear us say that we see our-selves involved in a healing ministry assume that is what we mean. It is strange how often the cultural forms of first century Palestine are simplistically transferred to the twentieth century West. We see healing going on in a variety of ways and on different levels. There are at least three levels: of individuals, of groups and of structures.

Over a period of time, the community house has become known as a place where some one would listen to problems and would help sort them out if they could. Consequently we have dealt with individ-ual problems often connected with the local housing situation, but ranging wide into many other areas of concern. We have occasionally put up homeless people. There have been complicated forms for the Department of Health and Social Security which we could help people fill in. There have been young people who have grown up in suburban Sheffield who did not know Pitsmoor existed, and who have been helped to an understanding of the whole of our society. We have even (despite ourselves!) helped more than one person to a good further degree and a high income on the strength of studying our area!

We have considered it very important to work alongside groups, and to help set up groups which would tackle things individuals could not take on. The neighbourhood group already mentioned is a good example. The 'case work' kind of approach, which suggests that you can somehow take an individual's problems and solve them or help him to solve them is clearly limited. The kind of pressures that are created by planning blight are important factors in many individual persons' breakdowns. The erosion of extended family ties through rehousing policy and mobility removes one of the vital support systems that helps individuals weather a problem and carry on. It also removes one of the most resonant arenas for ritual celebration of the passing of life. Even something as apparently trivial as the neighbourhood bonfire is in the decline, let alone celebrations of births and deaths. Yet the coming together of different generations, and the sharing of food, are as important a part of a November bonfire as of the most high-flown Eucharist. We feel strongly that any resurgence of community must be encouraged in such an area as ours, because the growing up of networks of knowing and caring is the only foundation for the health of the individual.

Just as individual health, like individual salvation, is a contradiction in terms, so it is insufficient to regard the problems of localities to be ultimately susceptible to self help projects. But any attempt to deal with structural problems can only begin from this local perspective. Pitsmoor is seen as being dependent on the rest of Sheffield, especially because it is an area of considerable social dislocation making great demands on the Community and Family Services Department (the social workers). Currently we are involved with the local Action Group in trying to persuade the Social Services to move into a closer relationship with people in the area they are meant to serve. We think that the present set-up encourages people to think of social welfare as something that can be manipulated by office-dwelling professionals, whereas a better picture is that of making some professional skills available to the local community through professional and voluntary social workers operating together from a local community base.

This can only happen when the gulf between social workers and recipients of social work is drastically reduced.

6. Taking Up the Cross and Following

The images of travelling and suffering have always been important in the faith. Often they have been perverted. Too often, Christians have only been allowed to travel with a select few, and real risk-taking has been absent. More seriously, any old suffering has been seen as a mark of Christ—which has unleased both maudlin sentimentality and appalling political apathy.

But if 'the way' is something people choose to be on, then only suffering which results from following that way has anything to do with the gospel. Equally, that 'way' is something that can be joined without naming Jesus himself. There are those who say 'Lord, Lord' but don't do anything (Luke 6: 46). There are those who care for the Christ in all men without naming him. Their deeds were his deeds. Matthew's story of the sheep and goats is the classic example of this (Matthew 35: 31).

It has always seemed right to work with any one who was going in the same way and to have no qualms about their particular sectarian stance. The Chairman of our Neighbourhood group is an ex-member of the Communist Party, and shames many Christians in his concern for local people and conditions. We also think it is important to open our front room for meetings of local groups whatever they are, if they have a need of somewhere to meet. There is of course nothing new in these demonstrations against a Christian ghetto mentality. But since that mentality still exists, it is important to argue that our approach is not a weakening of or an accommodation of the gospel, but an authentic gospel reaction in itself. If Christianity is seen as a once-and-for-all transforming innoculation, then it is logical, if offensive, to demand doctrinal purity. But in the gospels Christianity is seen as a way. It is possible to join or leave this 'way' at any time— the challenge is faced at every new decision. We are never irrevocably on the way or off it. It's a wager. We act *as though* Jesus is Lord, 'as if man had been born again'. The disciple's task is to follow, describe and indicate the way, pointing to the meaning of all things in Christ.

Some people see the way we have chosen, living in the inner city, as a way of suffering, because it's a rundown and stressful neighbourhood. We tend to find this attitude embarrassing, because we know people who have given up far more than we ever could, and live in far more stressful situations: and also because we are probably happier here than in a more salubrious area. I would certainly be suffering more in my previous role, teaching in a grammar school classroom, and would feel less free living in a semi in suburbia. So a more productive question to ask is, *what sustains us*, given that we could be in 'better' circumstances?

It is the support of the group in the house which has proved to be most important in this respect. The relationships which have formed over time have been both challenging and mutually supportive. The fact of making an intentional commitment with a group of like-minded people makes a major difference to living together. The idea of sharing was important at the opening of the house, but no decision was taken to pool all resources at that stage. It would have been difficult to envisage people risking that at the beginning of a temporary experiment. But an ethos of sharing has developed since that time which had to be built up slowly. It is generally the case that members' possessions are regarded as available for use by anyone else, given reasonable care. The only problem is knowing in whose room the thing you want is at the time. Similarly, friends who visit are visiting the community not just the individual. This is obviously not a rule. It just happens, and need not be thought remarkable, given the common catering. But it is certainly a source of enormous profit in the community. The amount of hospitality that is possible in a large household

83

that works together, means that large numbers of new friends, contacts, ideas, celebrations and joys are shared.

This sharing can also be the basis of support in times of trouble or stress. It is probably most clearly expressed in the worship of the house, where common concerns are voiced, and in the house meetings, at which business or policy decisions are taken. The worship of the house has taken many different forms appropriate to the time. When members have been working shifts, different forms have happened. We have sought to avoid one way of worship becoming a 'sacred cow'. At the moment, however, the eucharistic shared meal seems the most important image for us. We join once weekly in a formal short communion service in the early evening, a fortnightly Eucharist over Sunday lunch (in the Pitsmoor Study House), neither of which is only made up of house members. Once weekly, informal internal devotional sessions are held after 11 p.m., a time when most people can be expected to be around. Common concerns are raised in the context of a group of people who know each other well. We would fully expect this pattern of worship to change in the future as new residents come in.

The other really important way in which we are supported in what we do is our membership of Ashram Community. The four community houses which are at present part of the life of Ashram Community are only one aspect of that community's existence, although probably the most concrete manifestation of its life. But the Community numbers about one hundred and thirty people who together are searching for ways of expressing 'corporate Christian life and action in the world'. Without this body of people, and the innumerable local and long distance supporters, houses like this would not exist. More important, the fact that we are part of a wider community means that we are supported and challenged by others whom we also support and challenge. The agenda of families with mortgages and children at school is obviously different from younger single people living communally, as are most though not all house members. But there is a common concern to discuss and work towards responsible Christian lifestyles in a world of glaring poverty, which goes beyond charity donations.

Regular meetings between the families of the trustees of the house who hold it on behalf of the wider Community, and the 'family' in the house, are moving away from the business meeting to a more personal encounter. Support is also very practical—as when one trustee joined us in a battle with a landlord who was exploiting a local West Indian lady. The man used to come to the door and launch into a torrent of abuse at whoever opened it: in the end, we caught it, too—but a new home was found for the lady.

7. Proof-texting or Gospel-living?

I have tried in this exposition to use a couple of texts about the commissioning of the disciple group as a basis for a continuing theology of a group of people involved in common life and action according to the gospel of Jesus. The whole story has not been told, because it has not yet been played out. It is important, we feel, to see the story of Jesus' whole life as a dynamic framework, not a series of abstract concepts to which one must swear allegiance. This involves an understanding of the gospel which takes seriously the structure, movement, balance and integrity of the gospel accounts, and does not use them as a mine for proof texts, a basis for argument about the existence of a spirit world or any other such tangential activity. Our search is for an understanding of the gospels as 'faith texts', as stories which illustrate faith. And faith is precisely commitment to the Jesus whose behaviour in the world of first-century Roman-occupied Palestine was for his followers the clue to the whole universe and the clue to what each man could do next.

John Vincent's work in *Secular Christ*, summarized and pushed along in *The Jesus Thing*, seems to me to provide just such an understanding:

'Thus, every Jesus story begins with *incarnation*—getting where people are, living with them, sharing their lot. It goes on to *healing ministry*—listening to what people's real needs are, being the patient washer of feet or cleaner of streets or brewer of tea. It then with love and care, not breaking the bruised reed, will seek to lift out into the light the points, people, groups, happenings, which bring love, healing, acceptance, or significance: the ministry of *parables*. Then perhaps there will be specific actions: not great actions, but small, meaningful, planned, strategic actions, which are *acted parables*, prophetic signs, imaginative instances, which can liberate old elements in the situation, and hold up new possibilities. But all this will throw up and confirm the disciple group; it will force them together, and necessitate a discipline and a corporate mutual reliance. And perhaps there will be "polarisation", conflict, the parting of the ways, new alliances with strange bedfellows: *the cross*. And the cross is also the loneliness of the vicarious initiator, who "does his thing" because it is "everybody's". Then, finally, there might be signs of *resurrection,* as the deed catches on, or the new style evokes response, or the group is thrilled with a momentary success, or the disciple experiences "the joy of the resurrection". And occasionally, within the battles of history, he sees the *parousia,* the ultimate triumph of the Way. I believe that this theology *is* Christianity. Thus, I believe that it is what the churches should be embodying in their life in the future. Clearly, aspects of it have influenced churches in the past at various times: clearly, they do so now. But to attempt to re-design the whole resources of Christendom around this theological agenda would take more time than we have: though there are agencies where these agendas—or others very like them—are being pursued.'[11]

The call to discipleship is the call to join a group who will start at the beginning, with incarnation. This is an attempt to take seriously and afford dignity to a particular situation; not to escape upwards by spiritualizing, but to dig in by living alongside, and taking on the characteristics of life there. What this means in detail is therefore going to be different in different places. It is subject to no overall blueprint. Each time, people will have to find out what it means for them, and seek to avoid taking over the whole of the agenda of a situation while identifying themselves with the people there. Only when this is attempted can one begin to see what the gospel call to be *distinctive* could mean. Being distinctive is not a characteristic of the gospel in its own right. The distinctive parables and acted parables are going to be the issues or will be about the issues which will bring crucifixion, and over which resurrection if it comes will reign.

The end of my article arrives before the end of the story. I want to finish by underlining how parables can happen and am quoting from a letter written by some one who came to work on a playbus project and accepted temporary accommodation until she could find a flat, but decided to stay. Her experience of Christianity in South Africa—she is white—had made her suspicious. When she finally left, she wrote what seems to be a parable.

'. . . Funny how dead scared I was to go to Ashram. After getting the literature I pictured it as a cranky "religious" set up, way off beam. I liked what was said about living and working in the area, but was terrified at the prospect of living in a "religious" house. I decided there and then to stay only the minimum time. Just long enough to find a flat. That first week I was wandering around in a daze, waiting for the "religious fervour" to strike! What shock when it didn't! Something in the house kept me there—perhaps the atmosphere, which is concerned, friendly and warm, even to outsiders. The very fact that the house did not force any issues made me come to them myself in my own good time. I liked and like what the house is trying to do. I think it's extremely valuable, and did not realise the extent of its value until quite recently when I had become accustomed to the area, type of people and the moods of them—which you must admit are totally different to anything else. The people in Pitsmoor, Grimesthorpe and Attercliffe are different to any others anywhere, and have a charm and a pride all their own. A place where the door will be opened with a smile and the person will be accorded the respect and dignity they deserve just because they are human beings, is valuable. The fact that people come back proves that they feel the welcome and the acceptance.

I wondered right from the start what the house looked like to people outside, in the area, and I still don't know. I think some regard it as their last resort, some as a hole of do-gooders, and I hope some for what we wanted it to be. I can't work this out at all —perhaps to others it is a scapegoat. As for Mr. S., what a good and useful purpose it serves there, using up his venom and energy where it does least harm, instead of on his tenants! What it boils down to is that the house *is* there—it *is* used, and no matter how people see it it *is* a place to them. If they curse it, its an outlet for them. If they agree with it, it's a shelter. To each man it serves a purpose in his own mind. I'm sure some people see it as cranky and manned by 'useless communistic students', but I think once they get to know it and of it that image will change. As far as the actual house and occupants are concerned—all people are potential time bombs in one way or another liable to go off or sit and simmer. I am surprised there was not a lot more friction. It's a happy house, and you can feel it—personality clashes matter for only the few minutes they flare, and one is obliged to respect the other members for what they are and are not. We are all, after all is said and done, only products of our own environment and upbringing. It is necessary to have someone around as a shock-absorber and stabiliser . . . To be absolutely honest, I miss Ashram very much—I miss the teasing, laughing interchange, the noise that sometimes nearly drove me mad. I love the community life where there were three or four brains to pit yours against—having lots of people around—having loves and hates—laughs and tears in common.'

The story goes on, and inevitably goes up and down. Perhaps in the last resort only those who have observed it or been moved by it can talk theology about it. But, in the meantime, we go on telling our story—even our testimony—as a way of trying to retell the story of Jesus, and as a way to invite other people to join in on the act.

Notes

1. For more detail on Ashram Community Houses, see John J. Vincent, *The Jesus Thing,* pp. 78–80, 83–90. There are at present (1976) Houses in Rochdale, Sheffield, Middlesbrough and Kennington, London. Current information concerning the Community and the Houses can be obtained from the Community Office, 239 Abbeyfield Road, Sheffield S4 7AW. There is a tri-annual journal, *Act.*
2. Andrew Rigby, *Communes in Britain* (Routledge & Kegan Paul 1974), p. 9.
3. Ibid., p. 12.
4. Adolf Holl, *Jesus in Bad Company* (E. T. Collins 1972), pp. 15–16.
5. John H. Yoder, *The Politics of Jesus* (Grand Rapids: Eerdmans 1972), p. 112.
6. Adolf Holl, op cit., p. 83.
7. Austin Smith, C. P., *Passionist Inner City Mission* (49 Jermyn Street, Liverpool 8, 1975), pp. 18–19.
8. Edward S. Kessler, ed., *Deployment for Mission* (Urban Theology Unit 1975).
9. E. R. Wickham, *Church and People in an Industrial City* (Lutterworth Press 1957), p. 177.
10. Roger Garaudy, in *Salvation Today and Contemporary Experience.* Qtd. Pauline Webb, *Salvation Today* (SCM Press 1974), pp. 65–6.
11. John J. Vincent, *The Jesus Thing,* p. 60.

Story and Liturgy

The Christian religion has had, from the first, a profoundly sacramental character, and the Body of Christ has always been a liturgical community. The experience of salvation was originally integrally related to the eucharistic experience of resurrection and renewal which was so unexpectedly received by the disciples of Jesus after his death.

1. Resurrection and Testimony

The Christian eucharist was essentially a corporate action, celebrated when the disciples 'were all with one accord in one place', and it expressed what the Church essentially was, a royal priesthood offering to the glory of God, and in the name of mankind, the 'matter' of man's secular existence. It was thus characteristically a *thankoffering* in word and deed for the creative and recreative activity which they experienced in the world, and which came to them in quite a new way through the presence in Spirit of the Jesus in whose company they had been for three memorable years. In doing what he had told them to do when they met together for a meal, i.e. in *recalling* him, they enjoyed his real presence; and through this celebration they proclaimed the saving acts of God in the history of their nation, and looked forward to the consummation of all history in Jesus as the End. For the spiritual presence was the seal of the One who keeps his promises, in whose life they participated through the embodiment of his Word 'full of grace and truth'. The eucharistic presence was not a quasi-physical occurrence which anyone with sharp eyes might see: you had to participate in the liturgical action with all your heart and mind and strength in order to know the Lord's peace—and that knowledge was itself a divine gift, not a human achievement.

The disciples' experience of resurrection and renewal was felt to be also a commissioning to new responsibility: a demand to live in a new way, the way of self-sacrificing love, and a compulsion to preach a new message, the good news of new life in and through Jesus. In their preaching they were not concerned with making assertions for the benefit of Greek intellectuals, nor with telling wonders to compel pious Jews into the new Way: they were simply giving their testimony to a life-changing experience, affirming the truthfulness of the Jesus-way and inviting all to join them who were prepared to go through the baptismal sacrament of death and rebirth in order that they might be incorporated into the eucharistic community.

2. Obstacles and options

Such, in bare outline, is the 'permanent sacramentality' as Schillebeeckx calls it, which is intrinsic to the Christian religion. Massive in its range, it yet contains, in the way it has developed through history, three practical and theoretical difficulties which cause it to be a doubtful option for religious sympathizers, let alone for 'cultured despisers'.

First, there is the cultic setting of the Church's liturgical activity: it is most often acted out in special buildings which have been deliberately 'consecrated', i.e. set apart from secular use. These buildings usually contain abnormal furniture, and in them stylized antique costume is often worn.

Secondly, the liturgy expresses its controlling ideas through images and concepts which have become alienated, for the most part, from the contemporary 'experiential togetherness' in the secular world. These ideas are set in a pattern of thought and behaviour which continuously looks back into man's childish dependence upon a great Fixer of natural and historical events, whereas contemporary human culture looks forward into man's autonomous development of a new world through his own cultural, political and economic activity. These ideas are expressed moreover in language which tries (and fails) to be simultaneously evocative and categorizing.

Thirdly, the manner in which the ritual of the cult is done expresses a pattern of submission rather than appropriation, passivity rather than activity, imposition rather than participation.

There are three possibilities open to the radical at this point. In his desire to get to the root of the matter he can decide (i) that the tree of Christianity, impressive both for its longevity and the wide spread of its branches in the past, has now become hopelessly decayed, and must be pulled down and burnt; (ii) that the decay in the tree may yield to treatment, but it will take many years, and in the meantime some alternative living tree must become his shelter; (iii) that it is his business not to abandon the tree, and separate himself from the life which still runs weakly through it, but to take part in its treatment. The radical will remove fungus, he will cut out dead wood and superfluous growth, he will even engage in the risky business of root-pruning.

The first option has the attractiveness of all root-and-branch solutions, but the disadvantage of pulling up your roots and emigrating is that you may find yourself without a home, and whilst the fresh air of the secular world, unpolluted by the fog of theology, is at first attractive, it may turn cold and chill the homeless body. The second move has the attractiveness of a double option: you go to another home while someone else restores the old one for you, and in your own time you return and congratulate the workers—that is, if you wish to return at all. The third option carries all the praiseworthy overtones of Christian long-suffering, of 'quiet, brave endurance'. But we are not all heroes, and the risk of spiritual breakdown appears to be unduly high.

The first option I don't propose to consider further, on the ground that a man must find a spiritual home 'somewhere between Eden and the kingdom of God', and that to be homeless is a freedom which is ultimately absurd and tragic. What is involved in deciding between the second and third option?

3. Secular Worship

The setting of the Church's liturgy explicitly disjoins the sacred from the secular. Occasional worshippers, upon entering a church to take part in a service, display mental and emotional discomfort rather than interest and anticipation. They become somewhat less than human—defensive, resentful, shut in. In extreme cases, they become corrupt and their human dignity is thereby diminished. Regular worshippers, too, though familiar with the happenings in a church, and therefore able to avoid embarrassment, often show signs of alienation from normal human behaviour, until the service is all over. They are secular persons, and know themselves to be so, yet they ought (they think) to leave the world behind when they come into the House of God.

It may be replied that human beings ought to feel discomfort when they attempt to worship, for they are unworthy to do so, and are exposed to the life-changing influence of God's Spirit, which cannot but disturb before it reassures. This spiritual discomfort seems, however, to be a positive experience, and not to require participation in corporate worship for its benefits to be received. A human relationship, a conversation, an encounter with music or poetry or art, seems capable of yielding 'conversion', by which a person becomes totally available for others and, through them, for God. What seems to be at stake here is not whether people should feel discomfort or comfort in church, but why and how they do so. It is arguable that a misunderstanding of the nature of worship through its cultic setting causes a negative and unproductive discomfort, and so prevents spiritual growth and personal development.

Worship has often been practised as a denial of the secular by the sacred, as an attempt to enclose an area of acceptability which could secure the divine grace on a basis of a covenant-relationship. As a corollary, this attempt at enclosure carried an obligation to enlarge the area of the sacred and reduce that of the profane.

If, however, there is to be any effective connection between liturgy and life, surely it is essential to understand worship as in no way a contraction or denial of the secular. On the contrary, worship must integrate the allegedly profane and the supposedly sacred to make both genuinely secular. The profane must be corrected and consecrated, the sacred earthed and humanized.

There may be something to be learned here from non-Christian thought about worship. A. N. Whitehead, for example, for whom the ultimate reality was not a supernatural deity but 'events in their process of origination' regarded worship as the response of man to the total religious vision: 'worship is a surrender to the claim for assimilation, urged with the motive force of mutual love.'[1] Sir Julian Huxley, no friend to the churches, is prepared to acknowledge the value of worship within a naturalistic frame of ideas, not as a grovelling before a supreme Ruler, but as 'an opportunity for a communal proclaiming of belief in certain spiritual values, for refreshment of the spirit . . . for expressing in music or liturgy various natural religious emotions of praise, contrition, awe and aspiration, which would otherwise remain without adequate outlet'.[2] Finally, R. W. Hepburn, a humanist philosopher, writes: 'worshipping need not be seen as a submitting of oneself without insight to a wholly inscrutable will: need not be an unthinking, undiscerning adulation . . . worship can be the celebrating of moral perfection and beauty, fused in an intensifying strangeness. The worshipper can be exercising, not suspending, evaluative reflection. He is not purely passively accepting claims about the divine greatness and the divine will. He is actively recognizing them, rejoicing in them, responding to them. Thus his worship is not preface to a life of submission to commands from without: he extends, rather, the scope of his own moral judgements and moral vision. The sense of strangeness intimates to him that these can be extended indefinitely further—there is no final plumbing of the depths'.[3]

Since liturgical action is properly rooted and grounded in the life of the world, a living liturgy must begin with secular concerns, with the experience of love and hate, integration and disintegration, life and death. And since it is difficult to envisage a liturgy which employed as its main themes for the reinforcement of humanity the dark counterparts which diminish and destroy man—hate, disintegration and death—secular liturgy must begin in the places where ordinary people seek to celebrate events bearing love, integration and life. The specifically Christian festive themes, Harvey Cox suggests, 'can add depth, universality and compassion to secular celebration'; but they must never be artificially imposed: 'they are only properly introduced if they unlock, acknowledge and reassure'.[4] Here, clearly is the liturgical foundation of true secularity—the celebration of the world's life in all its possibilities and opportunities. Here too is the foundation of true religion—a form of community action which enables men to celebrate life as a gift whose true value has been clearly indicated by Jesus. The capacity to celebrate, says Cox, may be not merely a 'fringe benefit' for human beings, but an absolutely essential mark of their continuing humanity. Modern industrial man, Cox goes on, is so busy making history and making money that he misses the profound religious significance of festivity and fantasy. For festivity and celebration give him a necessary leisure from seriousness, and enable him to recover a true relationship with history, while fantasy liberates him for envisioning radically alternative life-situations, 'an activity of the mind which leads directly into political action against suffering and injustice'.[5] Genuinely secular liturgy is far from being a cosy ecclesiastical interest: it is an expression of cosmic thankfulness and the inspiration of cosmic concern. Through the Christian symbols of personal death and resurrection, of food and drink and sacrifice, comes the possibility of transforming society. For the hope of peace and justice upon earth is grounded in the making of an alternative society such as the Christian eucharist envisages and establishes.

4. Alien Forms

The second problem is the most complex of those identified. It is that in the traditional practice of Christian worship, the thought-forms have become alienated from the contemporary experience. The dogmatic assumptions which undergird the liturgy and the doctrinal formulae which are explicit in it must now expose themselves to having their truth-claims examined, and the language used in them must similarly be scrutinized for meaning or lack of it. We can approach this set of difficulties most usefully by drawing a distinction between 'affirmations' and 'assertions' in the expression of religious experience.

Liturgy receives its controlling ideas from the story which is rehearsed in it. Both historical perspective and internal order are given to liturgy by the 'story of stories' which shapes it. Story, in turn, depends upon liturgy for its communal acceptance and its power to conserve and transform society. A principal difference between religious story—be it myth, parable, autobiography, or biography— and scientific story is in the deeply personal character which belongs to religious story. The ingredients of scientific story—proposition, hypothesis, law, theory—are aspects of a control-system and, once established, they become impersonal instruments, whatever of human personality was put originally into their making.

At the heart of the Judaeo-Christian tradition is the personal story, a story of the actions of God experienced by men and celebrated in liturgy. Both the liturgy and the story are *affirmations*, personal testimonies to experience in the natural universe. A statement is being made as address passes into affirmation and back again. Indeed, the modern multivalent phrase 'making a statement', which can be used of a poem, a piece of music, a play or a dance, as well as of a declaration in verbal prose, expresses very well the multi-dimensional character of the Hebrew understanding of life.

Essentially, the Hebrew statement is about a mysterious uncontrollable presence in Spirit which discloses itself in events which have a life-giving or saving character. Yet it is not only the 'good' events which are so regarded: the Hebrew story fits in the 'bad' events like military defeat, economic recession, individual breakdown, even national exile, as well. These experiences represent an encounter with a force of personal judgement designed to save in the end by bringing men back to the truth about themselves and about the character of the universe in which they live. The 'bad' experiences are held in a creative tension with the mercy-revealing 'good' experiences in a story of One who will be there to save his people. This story can be contradicted, of course, by a story whose controlling idea is not cosmic benevolence but cosmic hostility, not cosmic meaningfulness but cosmic absurdity. No final resolution of this choice could be offered by an accumulation of evidence ordered by the procedures of inductive logic. The stories are present options which men are free to select by the criterion of whether they enhance their personal experience and reinforce their humanity—or not.

Affirmation and Assertion

The important difference between affirmation and assertion is that the *affirmation* expresses an existential understanding of personal involvement with the universe, whilst *assertions* attempt to give descriptive or explanatory information about the universe. An affirmation makes a claim, expresses a conviction, articulates a personal judgement or interpretation. Its objectivity can be checked in so far as it is communicable; it is this factor which keeps at bay the vagaries of individual impressions. Through systematic reflection on the appropriateness and implications of the claim, the conviction, the judgement, rational criticism is brought to bear on personal testimony. Christian theology is precisely this corporate critical reflection on personal testimony. Where the assertion aims to exclude alternatives, and is successful in so far as it does so, the affirmation allows for a legitimate ambivalence in attitudes. It has a strongly personal and provisional character, which accepts the limitations of 'This is true for me now' in contrast with the bold claim of 'This is true always and everywhere', in order to express what Philip Wheelwright has called the 'radical inseparability of meaningfulness and mystery'. Affirmation deliberately refuses, therefore, the challenge to establish empirically the causal link between divine and human activity; it simply accepts the paradox of double agency. This is where liturgy, considered as affirmation, is especially useful, for it is not restricted to verbal language: it uses the language of gesture and mime, it speaks through *action*. Whilst the four stages of the communion—taking, blessing, breaking and distributing—include the use of words, it is the actions which speak more clearly than the words. Here there is an integral connection between affirmation and action. What Sebastian Moore calls the 'eucharistic equation' (bread and wine = Body and Blood) 'is to be made at the level where it liberates and not at the empirical level where it merely puzzles'.[6]

5. Symbols—and God

The level at which the equation liberates is clearly the level of symbolic action and to a lesser extent of verbal symbols. The distinction needed here is between the verbal symbol which aims to be part of a control-system, namely, the concept, and that which is content to be part of a communion-relationship, i.e. the image. It is not possible here to go over the varieties of religious language, and in any case the subject has been covered very extensively in recent years, e.g. by Thomas Fawcett in *The Symbolic Language of Religion*.[7] It is no longer doubted that the language of science, for example, or of philosophy, is as symbolic as that of poetry and theology. The difference between these disciplines is predominantly in motive and method rather than in language. Where a control-system aims at the maximum of precision and of instrumental utility in its symbols, poetry, for example, while no less precise, is not concerned with utility, but rather with the expression of a vision, using images of wide range and evocative power. Where the concept seeks to eliminate alternatives, the image is inclusive, aiming to set up resonances on as many levels as possible, to evoke sympathetic participation rather than to set out a description or furnish an explanation. Thus, the attempt to translate image into concept in the interests of control will always de-nature the image while it fails to achieve the desired utility. To put the same point in different terms, the attempt to turn metaphors into models always reduces the power of the metaphor while it fails to achieve the instrumental virtue of the model.

The poet, by a process of creative synthesis that involves both clarification and growth, brings forward images to be the means of new discovery or new insight into the nature of reality. Both in the artist's creation and in the reader's or listener's apprehension, the *meaning* is in the closest possible unity with the words or the visual material. Thus, the artist creates a symbolic structure in which other persons, because of their rough similarity of mental constitution, can apprehend a nucleus of meaning. The important distinction to be made here is that whilst science is also in certain respects an artistic creation, needing and using metaphor, nevertheless, it is always trying to make the symbol objectively *denote* the character of an event or an object, i.e. to separate the meaning from the symbol, whereas poetry and arts seek to *connote* events or objects, to conjure them up or recall them to an audience, to furnish a new insight into their character and reality. Thus, whereas the audience of the scientist is disposed to take apart what he says, to analyse it, and to validate it empirically, the poet's audience is content to put together what he says in their own act of creation, their listening or their reading, to receive it whole and to validate it in terms of comprehensiveness, economy, elegance, consistency, fruitfulness.

Religious belief should therefore be regarded not as a theological instrument but as a summary of religious stories, stories which are told with the greatest weight and solemnity in liturgy. In this context of voluntary personal participation through initiation into the corporate activity of a religious community, the story invites worshippers to live in a universe of double meaning. As the late Austin Farrer put it in two luminous sentences, 'Our contemplation of God depends upon experience of his actions' and 'Our thought of God is the summary of a tale which narrates the actions of God'.[8]

To take myth as an example of a religious tale, it is clear that from the earliest times myth was integrally related with ritual, and likely that ritual preceded myth. Myth was not concerned with causes, explanations and theories, but with the conservation of society as orderly and meaningful. Moreover, it was primarily an emotional rather than an intellectual response to the mysterious forces of the natural universe, and its language was highly metaphorical, playing a creative role in the formation of personal experience. In view of Bultmann's well-known concern with de-mythologization, it is important to remember that his protest was directed against the presentation of myth as an *objective* world-view, as a set of assertions about the universe capable of falsification by empirical tests, and so liable to destroy a faith built upon it. Bultmann was not opposed, however, to mythological thinking for the right purpose and in the right context— a fact which some of his critics seem to have overlooked. In writing about the meaning of God as 'acting', Bultmann says that God's (supposed) action cannot be thought of as an event which is capable of objective, scientific demonstration in secular historical terms: God's actions can be seen only by the eye of faith as occurring *within* natural and historical events. He concludes: 'If someone now insists that to speak *in this sense* of God as acting is to speak mythologically, I have no objection, since in this case myth is something very different from what it is as the object of de-mythologizing. When we speak of God as acting, we do not speak mythologically, in the objectifying sense.'[9] Similarly, to speak of God as creator is not only possible but necessary, provided that the man who affirms it understands that he is making an existential confession not a cosmological assertion. Such an affirmation 'cannot be made as a neutral statement, but only as thanksgiving and surrender'.[10]

If assertions are impossible, affirmations are both possible and necessary, and when liturgical expression is given to feelings of cosmic awe, communion or thankfulness, it is affirmations that are being made. In this form, they are their own meaning and justification. The experiences and their liturgical affirmation occur perfectly naturally, and do not *entail* a supernatural type of explanation. Cosmic thoughts and feelings can be properly and beneficially articulated in symbolic actions and words without the notion of a supernatural deity: they can simply be expressed without being referred.

God

It is now open to us, therefore, to re-mint the principal 'organized symbol' of religion—the word 'God'—in such a way that whilst respecting earlier forms of using the word, we can be open to the Spirit's guidance how we should use it now. In particular, we can be liberated from the obligation to pay our addresses to William Blake's Nobo-daddy, a talking idol 'up there' whom we fabricate for ourselves in order that he may perform actions approved by us and to our satis-faction. We are free to recognize that the word 'God' does not stand for a personal being whose existence and activity can be objectively established. When we consider religious experience, and examine exclamations of 'God' and exclamatory address directed to 'God', it is evident that these arise out of personal situations of an ultimate character, and that the word 'God' is properly regarded as a semantic marker for experiences of ultimacy. We can then suggest that 'God' functions also to point to the sense of a quasi-personal presence con-fronting man in his secular existence, a presence which is entirely uncontrollable by man, and about whom assertions are impossible, because there is no means of checking their validity.

Our worship, our thanksgiving and our surrender may with free dignity be given to the living God in the world. In the words of Schillebeeckx: 'Acceptance of God is the ultimate, precise name which must be given to the deepest meaning of commitment to this world . . . the building up of the world into a community of persons in justice and love appears on closer reflection—or, more precisely, in a "dis-closure situation"—to coincide with acceptance of God and, in the concrete, even with faith in God.'[11]

Anyone who attempts to participate in corporate worship must be prepared to use his imagination, and to respect the cultural tradition of the liturgy in which he opts to join. He must have sufficient patience to understand and accept the variety of religious experience which a worshipping community deploys. Further, in the practice of theology, that communal exercise in clarification and evaluation in which secular man shares his experience with the symbols of Transcendence, he can help the other members and they can help him, as they reflect together on the dialectical relation between their varied experiences with their different content, and the equally varied and different verbal forms of articulating these experiences.

Speech and Silence

For this purpose personal testimony and religious story must be considered more significant and more meaningful than theological proposition.

Even testimony and story will not communicate the whole of an individual's or a group's religious activity, for the verbal symbols of human speech are not adequate to the task. In this sense, actions speak louder than words, which means that liturgical action will speak more clearly than liturgical texts, just as liturgical texts are more illuminating than doctrinal statements. This is important not only from the viewpoint of a phenomenology of religion, but also from a sense of the limitations of the human capacity to verbalise experience. For the rest there is silence—which is not the same as speechlessness. For speechlessness may be the consequence of being dumbfounded (loss of speech) or of technical incapacity (lack of speech). But silence, which can only be meaningful for beings who do have the power of speech, and which may be momentary or reflective, may indicate a *refusal* of speech. As such, it is often genuinely communicative.

6. Purging the Symbols

It does not follow, however, that rationality should be abandoned by religion. It is the task of reason, as Whitehead put it, to 'understand and purge the symbols'. Because of the richness and fertility of religious symbols, only rational criticism can save religion from credulity and superstition. If religious stories are not critically examined, there is no prospect of their being validated for faith. What kind of test would be appropriate to establish that religious utterances are anything more than expressions of individual taste, a record of subjective impressions which tell us something about the individual believer but nothing more? The criteria of artistic truthfulness, not those of scientific truth, will be the ones we need. For liturgy, as we have seen, is an artistic creation, an existential affirmation of a pattern of personal involvement with Transcendence. The religious poet, the greatest maker of liturgy, is unable to give us new information about an unseen world, because no adequate means exist for verifying or falsifying his statements. He may well give us new insights, however, by drawing attention to resemblances or contrasts which we had not previously noticed, and so give us a *new imaginative slant* on the everyday world. But 'unless "truth" is to be used as an honorific title for the impressiveness of what a great poet may show about (say) the Christian symbols—their astonishing comprehensiveness, flexibility, power to evoke the profoundest feeling—we must deny that imaginative insight even on this scale is enough to establish more than meaningfulness and possibility'. 'Thus, a poem may be "true" in that it reveals an "internal necessity", a "convincing shapelessness"; it may be a "sincere expression of opinions sincerely held", or it may make us see an object as we have never seen it before—but it will not tell us about the real existence of anything in or beyond the universe.'[12]

If this is correct, an important consequence follows for the use of creeds in the liturgy. It is well known that the Church managed without a creed in the eucharist for almost 800 years, this test of loyalty and orthodoxy being properly reserved for the services of Christian initiation. Yet even in this context there is a risk of misunderstanding and misuse. For the earliest Christian confessions, as we have them in the New Testament, are either personal testimonies, set in preaching or teaching, or they are Christological hymns. In other words, they articulate thanksgiving and surrender, and they do not purport to be objectifying assertions: if they were, their use in worship, the very antithesis of a control-system, would be quite impossible. Considered as testimonies or forms of address, however, they are useful and legitimate summaries of Christian conviction, and may be expressed in liturgy and story. We have to be prepared to let such 'organized' symbols work, and not be distressed when they do not; and if it seems probable, over a period of time and through a developing consensus in the Church, that some of the symbols or images have died, then without despair or panic we must set about finding or creating new ones. The great biblical metaphors of God were developed in a cultural context very different from the sophisticated urban setting in which many people now live: the fact that these images have lasted as long as they have ought to be a matter of thanksgiving; but we should not feel bound to them as if they were sacrosanct. The same is true *a fortiori* of the models of Hellenistic philosophy in which Christian testimonies have become petrified.

The Tent and the Temple

Is it not possible that the 'death' of God has been caused by boredom as much as by assassination? What we need is not new ideas so much as new energy. That is why in our present situation of wistful helplessness moral exhortation leaves us unmoved and linguistically purified assertions have no power to inspire us. What we need is a restoration of our energy. That can only be achieved as we offer ourselves for initiation into the pentecostal liturgy of a quest, open ourselves for celebration of the gift of life, a celebration which combines festivity and fantasy in a constantly renewed experience of resurrection and renewal—and all in an unreserved acceptance of our secularity and our tragic freedom. It is precisely this kind of celebration, with all its religious, moral and historical implications, that the continuing Christian Church offers as a service to mankind.

But it can only offer this service if it is prepared to abandon the Christian attempt to fix the God who continually surprises us. There is always a tendency for rituals to retain myths even when the myths have lost their vitality. Revision is therefore a permanent requirement for living liturgy if it is not to become alienated from contemporary culture; the alleged benefits of unchanging worship, namely, religious stability and liturgical security are almost always bought too dear. No doubt, the tension between the Tent and the Temple will always be with us. If people must leave the Temple and go to the Tent in response to the Spirit's radical call, then go they must; but if they can remind the Temple-dwellers that they are still a pilgrim people, and that the Temple itself is merely an advanced base, not a permanent halt, whilst themselves remaining in the Temple, better still.

7. Free to Celebrate

Whether our worship be carried out in the Tent or the Temple, four conditions must be present: first, contemporary worship demands real congregational participation and a new pattern of liturgical leadership which reduces the monopoly of the ordained ministers; secondly, liturgy must be flexible enough to allow re-examination of its assumptions and its performance, its story and its ritual; thirdly, liturgy must rediscover its original festive character in order that unself-conscious celebration may be enjoyed; fourthly, worship must be so firmly grounded in secular history that its material provides the possibility of integration and reconciliation on all levels of personal activity. The whole range of the Jesus-deeds must be illuminated and expressed in the Christian liturgy for the re-making of the world.

It is arguable that 'man-who-thanks' is the most natural man of all, since by the perpetual thankoffering of his secular existence before Transcendence he realizes his authentic being as the priest of creation. Whether he offers his worship within an institutional mainstream church or in a neighbourhood domestic para-church must, in a secular society, be a matter of free choice. If the churches continue to believe that the catholic tradition is the way of truth, let them continue to work at the possibility of opening up the eucharistic experience so that it becomes profoundly experimental and forward-looking as well as profoundly traditional and historical. There is no head-on conflict here. A living church can well afford to be flexible in its liturgical pattern, to provide *both* kinds of opportunity for contemporary people to celebrate the gift of life and participate in their own 'story of stories'.

Radical Renewal

It is precisely here that the practical decision has to be made between going (temporarily?) and staying, i.e. between the second and third options which we suggested earlier,[13] and it is just here that the failure of the Church—to undertake a *radical* renewal of its liturgical action—not merely of its texts, but of its whole cultic pattern—bears most heavily upon the members. This is the point at which a simple and domestic, but intimate and powerful, *agape* in someone's living room, leading into various activities under the heading of 'community care', is claimed not only to be more genuinely secular than a church service, but more eucharistic than the church's eucharist. I do not think we can deny the force of this testimony. Must the two things be mutually exclusive? There are dangers as well as benefits in small-group activity, but if I am honest, I have to admit that unless a Christian is prepared to shop around for meaningful worship and is lucky enough to find it, he will be much better employed in a para-church than in no church. And it will do no good for churchmen to bring in the loyalty argument at this point: most churchpeople have been passively loyal to the Temple for too long: only the active possibility of moving forward with the Tent, in full acceptance of the problems of continuous change, will maintain them in Christian service at all. In the Tent we are unlikely to claim that we have arrived, or that we know: in the Temple it is all too easy to do both.

What preserves the identity of the Church is that the mystery of promise continues to give itself in history—our history. If it were not so, we should go in danger of missing 'the truth that is always coming'. Thus it is possible, with an open approach which takes the risks in the name of the transforming Spirit, to respect and be thankful for the past history of Christianity, above all for the revolutionary living and preaching which were centred upon the original eucharistic experience of resurrection and renewal in Christ. We can then move on to pursue our obligations to present society and the world of the future by making our science and technology into a thankoffering for consecration by the mysterious and powerful Presence who gives salvation. Then too the Church is liberated for its true role, that of the priestly community which offers the life of the world and its own life for the world.

Notes

1. *Science and the Modern World* (Mentor Books), p. 172.
2. *Religion without Revelation* (Max Parrish, 2nd ed., 1957), p. 26.
3. Ronald Hepburn, 'The meaning of Life', in *The Listener*, 2nd Feb., 1967, p. 162.
4. *Feast of Fools* (Harvard University Press 1969), p. 81.
5. Ibid., pp. 86, 87, 110.

6. Sebastian Moore and Kevin Maguire, *The Dreamer not the Dream* (Darton, Longman and Todd 1970), p. 28.
7. SCM Press 1970.
8. *Faith and Speculation* (A. and C. Black 1967), pp. 32, 35.
9. *Jesus Christ and Mythology* (SCM Press 1960), pp. 61–2.
10. Ibid., pp. 63, 69.
11. Edward Schillebeeckx, *God the future of Man* (Sheed and Ward 1969), p. 76.
12. R. W. Hepburn, 'Poetry and Religious Belief' in *Metaphysical Beliefs* (SCM Press 1957), pp. 119–31.
12. See pp. 90–1.

SIX

JOHN J. VINCENT

Christian and Radical

1. A Christ-centred Radicalism?

This book records 'stirrings', not attempts to build underwater cities. It was written by people who heard what each other was saying, and felt it to be roughly in the same piece of ocean. The book does not come from a group of people who have agreed on what is to be believed or lived by. So that any attempt to put us all in the same basket would be repudiated by each one of us, for different reasons!

Yet it is not accidental that we have individually said what we have said, and it is worth looking at it again, and developing some of the lines further, to see where they might lead. In fact, we have already had a chance to begin this task, so that I can also add some account of what happened, when the chapters were worked over by a larger group, at the 'Contemporary Theology' Conferences of 1973 and 1974, described in *New City*,[1] and at the further one held in 1975.

Before doing this, however, it is perhaps worth asking whether the slogan 'Christ-centred Radicalism' is worth using. What we mean by it can only be gathered by considering what each of us individually has said. But what of the slogan? Can it be used to clarify rather than confuse? I believe it can.

'Radicalism' tends to be used by every man to mean his own 'thing'. It is probably too late to alter this; and probably it would be a mistake to try. Literally, it means 'that which goes to the roots', based on the Latin *radix*, root. But that does not take us very far. So let me say that our use of the term is meant to indicate several basic elements, which seem to be found in any sort of radicalism.

First, a radicalism springs from *a thoroughgoing and basic stance of such a character as to be clearly orientated around one particular world view, teaching or philosophy*. Thus, it is certainly proper to speak of radical conservatism, radical Marxism, and radical Christianity. The debate is then about whether the stance is proper or authentic. In each case, the attempt is made to get back to the primitive or essential form of the view in question. Perhaps it is its earliest form, or its latest; certainly it will be its most thoroughgoing and idiosyncratic. Radicalism in this sense is an attempt to return to the

105

distinctive genius of particular views. It is distinguished from liberalism, syncretism or compromise, simply because of this thorough-going stance based on taking one particular starting point with complete seriousness.

Secondly, radicalism *has some immediate practical and secular distinctiveness and implication for the whole of life.* It is not merely a philosophy or an opinion. It shows itself in commitment, practical experimentation, and action. A radicalism is a total life-style which differentiates itself by its completeness from the contemporary *milieu* and the surrounding ethos. This is, again, true whether one is speaking of a philosophical, political or religious radicalism.

Thirdly, *radicalism is extremism, single-mindedness, at times narrow-mindedness.* A view is not radical if it merely takes over the dominant mind-set of the time and shows how the starting-point in question can be accommodated to it. A radical Marxism is not a revisionism; and a radical Christianity is not a revisionist Christianity. Particularly in our time, it appears from outside as a happy, self-conscious and self-consistent worldview, even a 'ghetto' mentality. It acts on the assumption that all men will not, and perhaps should not, became radicals. It is based also on the conviction that radicalism can only help by 'doing its own thing', by 'being its own self', and by making its contribution to the whole by so doing and being. In fact, the radical believes that his way is the *true* way for *all*. But he can only show this by being and doing it on his own, for the sake of all.

By speaking of a 'Christ-centred' radicalism, it is argued that there are people who make 'Christ' the centre for a thoroughgoing and basic stance orientated around him, who take this Christ-stance into practical and secular action, and who are prepared that this shall set them off in more or less distinctive ways from other elements in their society.

Clearly, all this would have implications in terms of ethical, social and economic attitudes on the part of individuals and groups which are quite beyond the bounds of this book. The study of contemporary radical Christianity is still in its infancy, and the scene, outwardly at least, is confusing.[2] All that has been here attempted has been to suggest a variety of 'ways in', whereby Christians can get at the basic element—the 'Christ' element, which stands behind and is prior to the radical Christian groups—or some of them. Everyone calling himself a Christian radical would not agree on our position. It is for this reason that we have used the term 'Christ-centred', which denotes a *restrictive* as well as a more specific form of Christian radicalism.

Some common elements of 'ways in', we found, have emerged

within this 'Christ-centred radical' view, at least as we have attempted to do our work and listen to each other. Such elements are not a 'consensus' of what has been said already in the various chapters. Rather, they comprise one more attempt to 'get it all together', based on listing and developing some of the dominant elements which, at least to me, characterize the mood and content of the individual contributions. They do not, I hasten to add, represent what we all agree on. Rather, they comprise one final fling at getting out what we think we are on to!

2. The Jesus Story

An insistence upon the Jesus of the gospels is our invariable starting-point. Jesus is the only central and 'given' element in Christian faith. Liberal and humanist Christianity was often embarrassed by it, evangelical and catholic Christianity did not need it. But for the Christ-centred radical, the synoptic gospels' picture of Jesus Christ is the very basis of the Christian 'thing'. Even in terms of observation, Jesus is the *only* constant element in the pluralism of Christian theologies, cultures and denominations. Christians function 'as if' Jesus was decisive and determinative; this is what makes them 'Christians'. So the gospel account of Jesus forms a starting-point, and, arguably, a point for criticism and even judgement of theologies. Even if there are many Jesuses, still a debate with common referrents is possible. And even though the 'edges' of the historical Jesus or the Christ of Faith are not always clear, yet there are more or less agreed 'frontiers'. It is possible to know that one is not referring to *nothing* when one refers to Christ. And that means that there is a proper and endless debate about historical, ecclesiastical, symbolic or mythical origins of sayings, about what is central and what is peripheral, what is truly implied and what can only be read in, in this writer and that, and what we can make of it all today. Yet, in the end it is not the case that references to Jesus Christ are meaningless, irresponsible or contentless. Criticism has often been an excuse for ignoring Jesus.

Our observation is that there has recently been a convergence of theological concern upon the figure of Christ, which we do not believe has been developed. As yet, we have not used the insights of *Christology* to answer the decisive and determinative questions of Christianity, like, What is Humanity? What is Personal Existence? What is Community? What is God? What can be done in History? Instead, it seems to us, we have allowed Jewish and pagan ideas of these matters to be continued, without asking *what* humanity, personal

107

existence, community, 'God' or history could ever be 'implications' or 'predicates' of Jesus. Thus, our demand is that Christians should not only be reconciled to the fact that they have to deal with Jesus, but also begin to think again from that point.

This demand for a reopening of the Jesus question carries with it an insistence that we take the Jesus *story* seriously. Thus we have a concern to *remythologize*, and a new hope for myth. The gospel story becomes 'myth' when it is taken as life-determining and ultimately significant. 'Myth' is thus the secret of life. John Davies remarks on the powerlessness of Death of God radicalism, and the *power* of myths to move men to action. Similarly, Tytler speaks of stories which 'present options which men are free to select by the criterion of whether they enhance their personal experience and reinforce their humanity—or not.' Thus you may *choose* your myth; *affirm* the myth that seems already to be operative in you; or even affirm the *ritual* which embodies the myth.

In our Conferences, we discovered that one of the problems with all this was that the stories from the gospels tend to leave many people cold. Many of the stories seem meaningless to us. So that the *use* of the Jesus element is a vital question, which recurs throughout our work. *Stories only need to be set down about events which have happened.* The stories of Jesus sustain faith within the group or individual that wishes to live with them. They do not normally bring outsiders to faith. And we would, in fact, also say that the stories are not the evangelism. The action about which stories have to be told is the evangelism. This will be more explicitly developed in a moment.

Ed Kessler and Roy Crowder show the value, rather than the limitation, of the dependence of Christianity on a historical story/ myth. There is a debate about *myths* which the Christians with their story badly need to 'get in on'. People are entitled to ask 'What is the result of your myths?'. Some might ask, 'What are the theological myths that help in, say death and tragedy?'. People need to be able to say, 'These myths are good, and those myths are bad'. There are false myths all around us—the myths of white paternalism which means racism, western superiority which means exploitation, economic *laissez-faire* which means injustice. We must ask what myths from the Christian's story support these false 'myths'. There are false Christs and false prophets. The debate must be especially about what our stories are *heard* to be saying by people with desperately pressing needs. And we must hear what people with desperately pressing needs are actually *using* from the gospel stories. We need to 'get a nose' for both. Without it, theology is sterile. With it, theology is at least vitally related to what is happening in the whole life of man—which means vitally related to certain groups or nations at certain stages in their existence; or to certain individuals or families at certain stages in theirs. Roy Crowder's piece is a significant start from one group.

The fact that this in our time has led to a crop of theologies featuring Jesus as liberator, or as black messiah, or as revolutionary, or as friend of the deviant, or as champion of youth against establishment, is more a matter of rejoicing for us than it might be for others. At least people with pressing agendas are finding elements from the gospel which can aid them. There is only a difference in degree between what such groups make of Jesus, and what the Christian denominations have made of him, or what the existentialist, psychological, evangelical, catholic, or liberal-humanist interpretations made of him. In every case, *the interpretation lives for as long as there are people living by it.* In every case, the interpretation will survive or fall by the 'consensus of the faithful', but 'the faithful' in a time of pluralism do not agree—and this is good. It is urgent that there be more theological advocates of this group enthusiasm or that. The theologian should not presume to take the part of history, and judge prematurely between the parties. Happily, no theologian exists who is outside cultural, social, political, racial and denominational predeterminism, so that, we must hope, no theologian will attempt also to be a 'reconciler' or 'peacemaker'. The theologian's task is both more exciting and more elusive—to hear the stories actually being told out of the gospels and out of contemporary secular existence, and to tell them again with their theological significance more plainly shown. Only after many more stories, and many more apparently irreconcilable Jesus-images and Jesus-myths, will the theologian be needed again as a 'systematizer'.

3. Theology as Action-theology

Theology arises from *action*. Theology is 'the communal exercise in clarification and evaluation in which secular man shares his experience with the symbols of Transcendence' (Tytler). Theology is 'response to events' (Davies), the Bible is 'events, words, concepts and judgements, always given with hindsight' (Alistair Kee). Thus a variety of human actions constitute 'faith' in Davies's five gospel stories: 'the insight, boldness and persistence to convert concern into effective action', 'responding to the overwhelming pressure to be thankful, come what may', 'confidence in your own status as a child of God', 'recognizing the subtle, canny kind of authority which Jesus exercises', and 'a willingness to be surprised'. Therefore, 'theology is basically about things which happen to people: it is about stories', so therefore what we need is people doing things, so that they might tell stories about their happenings afterwards. 'It is what Christians do that tells us what they are' (Donald Tytler). Religious belief is only one aspect of religious activity. The most distinctive things the Christians do are to engage in 'secular worship', that is, live 'the way of Jesus', and engage in 'eucharistic celebration', that is, 'offer to the glory of God, in the name of mankind, the "matter" of man's secular existence'. The story in liturgy is 'affirmed' in action, and 'speaks through action'. Here, *concepts*, verbal symbols which aim to be part of a control system, are less useful than *images*, which are 'content to be part of a communion-relationship'. We need metaphors, not models. The gospels offer us a mass of myths, parables, and stories crying out for sacraments and quasi-sacraments.

Thus, we see the future of theology as 'reflection after revelation'. There is a more or less implicit agreement that Christian theology does not happen when theologians get together and share their beliefs, but rather happens when Christian disciples get together and share their experiences. As Tytler says, 'what we need is not new ideas so much as new energy'—and 'the dynamic quality of story and liturgy' give this. Thus, 'doing theology' is Christians sharing their stories—the specimens, models and paradigms out of which they have made their life meaningful. 'Theology is not a description of timeless truths, but a description of what goes on in Christianity.' The Bible does not theologize; it tells stories. Stories, 'creative, true and healing myths' are what biblical men lived by, and what we need to live by (John Davies). Some striking recent words of Walter Hollenweger may be quoted as a further instance of this point of view: 'Taken seriously, this offers a real possibility of discovering a methodology of theology in an oral culture where the medium of communication is—just as in biblical times—not the definition, but the description; not the statement, but the story; not the doctrine, but the testimony; not the book, but the parable; not the *summa theologica,* but the song; not the treatise, but the television programme.'[3]

In the Conferences, we reflected on the way in which *stories precipitate gospel*. In the gospels, there is a process; first, an activity of Jesus; second, an activity of the disciples; third, there are social and personal effects and results; finally, society's assumptions are upset and new social patterns emerge. Then someone comes and writes it all down. But the records are secondary to these things happening. The world *had* been turned upside down. We have neglected the relation of gospel to church history. If there is no story to tell, then there is no need for theology. The only unique thing about a man is

110

his own history. So we must get on creating the history—it could be gospel. All we must do is get back into making the story. John Davies declared that 'Radical theology will be assessed in terms of its effectiveness in enabling theological practitioners'. Theology should be 'enabling practitioners', that is, giving people the tools with which they can do theology. For this 'doing theology' cannot be done in an academic setting; it can only be done where people are experiencing the tragedies, joys, confusions, deceptions and triumphs of actual faith-life. In passing, this itself means a new assessment of *where* theology is best done, and *where* the theological expertise of the churches should be located.[4]

All this adds up to a new regard for *testimony*. What Christians can be heard to be *doing with their stories* is significant. What they do with them might be (1) to act in the light of them, (2) to worship or act communally in the light of them, and (3) to tell stories or give witnesses and testimonies about the way the truths contained in them actually 'work' for them. Our Easter Conference in 1973 determined that it would be our main concern for 1974 and 1975 to find out how theology and gospel were actually being used in some specific situations. In this sense, belief is a *consequence* of religious activity. Personal testimony and religious story precipitate theological propositions.

In the event, the stories we studied in 1974 and 1975 were as numerous and varied as the people present. Clearly, the stirrings in the Christian camp are not only in our imagination. From the Philippines, we learned of some striking contemporary gospel stories from a consultation on 'Doing Theology' held in Manila in 1972.[5] From Geneva, we heard of the stories coming out of Urban-Industrial Mission agencies in touch with the World Council of Churches.[6] From Christians participating in change, we heard of political and social action based on the gospel.[7] From areas of ecumenical experiment, we heard of gospel elements battling against structures, even newly formed ecumenical ones.[8] From Urban Theology Unit's own ecclesiastical 'patch', we heard of gospel elements in a newly created institution, the Sheffield Inner City Ecumenical Mission.[9] From Tyneside and elsewhere, we heard of gospel notes at work in community development and grass-roots neighbourhood politics and planning.[10] From the charismatic/evangelical and the community/radical wings of the churches, we heard of similar dominant gospel motifs at work.[11] From South Africa, others; from South America, others again.[12]

It is too early to do more than refer the reader to places where he can ferret out such stories—and to encourage him to write his own.

We merely record that the gospel is alive as a living dynamic in men's creative self-interpretation; and observe some of the things which follow from this for theology.

4. Faith as Action-commitment

A new understanding of *faith* follows from the two main points so far. Davies, Tyler and I each develop this. All of us see faith not so much as believing in the existence of transcendent beings or realities, but rather as actions based on certain stories or myths. In Tytler's words, faith has to do with *affirmation*, which 'makes a claim, expresses a conviction, articulates a personal judgement or interpretation', rather than *assertion*, which 'attempts to give descriptive or explanatory information about the universe'. Our view distinguishes faith from belief, and sees faith as some kind of commitment, 'blik', or stance. 'Faith' as 'belief' is usually 'in something', usually something which gives security, especially if it is a group 'deviance' which is exciting or unusual. But faith itself is essentially a commitment, a leap in the dark, a decision, an action, a piece of discipleship based on certain stories or around a certain person. It is 'the dynamic response and commitment emanating from situations within life which call for concrete deeds,' and which 'proleptically' lead into an unknown future. According to Davies, faith is 'openness to new possibilities'—represented by Jesus in the gospel stories, or by God in the Abraham story. Both James and Paul agree that faith appears as action, though action based not on law but on love, or Christ, or God—or, even better, simply on 'faith itself' as the propellant or point of departure.

This concentration of Christian hope in human and secular action and commitment gives us *optimism*—an optimism that everything is going *for* us, and not, as most disillusioned churchmen seem to think in this obviously post-Christian and post-theological age, that everything is going *against* us. Crowder happily leaves behind establishment expectations, and rejoices in the gospel story in places of need in the inner city.

Tytler's assessment of liturgical action is optimistic: Christianity exists so long as people are acting the story. Kessler's analysis is optimistic: faith is taking place outside the Church all the time. We all see hope in recent theology leading to Jesus. I have hopes for a 'post-theistic' Christianity. We thus stand for an affirmation of the way things are, a preparedness to welcome and live with our world of contemporary secular oddities—Jesus fascination, occultism, drugs, *Godspell*, *Superstar*, ritualism and superstition, anti-establishmentism, 'doing your own thing', charismatic movements, radical movements, commune movements. We affirm this apparently mad and mutually irreconcilable pluralism. We think it is good. And as Christians we have more hope from it than we ever had from the establishment Christianity of 'main-line Christendom'.

But, of course, our confidence is also based on our understanding of Christianity. We have a new confidence that Christianity gives us clues and meanings into 'the way things really are'—clues only now emerging because we affirm our secular times. With us all, it is into history and the nature of humanity, with Crowder it is into 'what is really there' in human existence, with Davies it is into the kind of people who are the faith-people in every culture, with Tytler it is into a transcendent universe of meaning, with Kessler it is into the true value of human interaction, with myself it is into the force and possibility of a new life-style.

There is also agreement between us that there is no one 'thing' which is revealed. Rather, the revelation of the clue and meaning will be discovered only when one is committed in faith to doing what the Jesus story seems to be saying to one, and reflecting on this and testifying to it in the community of the 'faith-ful'. To be a Christian is to 'live in a universe of double meaning' (Tytler), acting as if what is only a clue were in fact plain for all to see, living as if the story which one has opted for were really the story which has claimed the whole universe for itself. We do not any longer see ourselves as persuading everybody concerning the rationality of the faith. Indeed, we see the over-anxious, punctilious attempts of the last hundred years to reduce Christianity to a discovered rational 'essence' as the greatest mistake. Even though each of us has his own shorthand for that 'essence', we all see that shorthand as temporary expedients, rather than permanent dogmatic statements. We see that 'people believe that history has a meaning which is not yet fully disclosed' (John Davies), and as Christians want to follow that belief wherever it leads.

Inevitably, this approach will multiply the diversity and plurality within Christendom. The question of doctrinal consensus is itself a major problem. *Solidarity* is a good thing between Christians, but how far solidarity is in fact aided or prevented by people all thinking the same is worth debating. If one listens to young Christians from Sri Lanka, or Chicago, or Bolivia, or Botswana, one can hardly avoid the conclusion that what is labelled 'Christian' by each is widely divergent in terms of background, content, intention and 'values'. The use of common language—salvation, liberation, reconciliation, wholeness, kingdom of God, and so on—does not mean that there is a

113

common point of reference. We need much more detailed and patient study of *what use Christian categories are actually put to*. The emerging 'sociology of theology' will help in this, it is to be hoped. Meantime, we insist that theology always has been 'action-theology' when it has been authentic—as it invariably has at the *point of origin* in a specific piece of action-commitment. The 'problem' of consensus only emerges when what people get out of the gospel becomes systematized and has to be reconciled with the witness of others. It is a *necessary* problem. But its solution gives us second-hand, not first-hand theology.

5. God as Predicate

Explicitly in the papers of Tytler, Davies and myself comes the demand that speech about 'God' can and must only now be done as a secondary procedure after speech about Jesus. The proper question is not what must Jesus have been in order to be 'Son' to an already conceived 'God', but rather, what 'God' must there be who has Jesus as a 'Son'? Hence, we speak of God as an implication along the way; as the one who stands at the end of the way, as the *predicate* to all that for which Jesus is subject, and to all actions in which Jesus as subject enters into activity. As Tytler says, 'the word "God" is properly regarded as a semantic marker for experiences of ultimacy', which also functions 'to point to the sense of a quasi-personal presence confronting man in his secular existence, a presence which is entirely uncontrollable by man, and about which assertions are impossible, because there is no means of checking their validity'.

This problem of the 'God' concept is the theme of my own essay, in which I suggest that, for contemporary man at least, 'God' as a 'marker' in modern usage has not been a *possible* concept. The Christian's way must be in a no-man's land between the traditional God-worshippers on the one hand, and the atheists on the other. The New Testament can assist us precisely here. We must 'universalize' on the basis of the events of Jesus, not in the 'divinity' direction, but rather in the 'secular-universalistic' direction. In our time, the decisive question is 'the discovery of significant Jesus-existence now', and we must live with commitment to Jesus before we can discover whether 'God' is possible again—and which 'God'. At the Conferences Alistair Kee came in here : Jesus is not the incarnation of God, but the incarnation of 'the way of transcendence'. He (Kee) wishes to speak of transcendence, not as a concept similar to that of 'God', but rather as an experience, that of 'transcending'. In fact, by identifying trans-

114

cendence with a transcendent God, God has become entirely immanent: defined, comprehended, available and predictable. Meantime, transcendence has become alien from secular man, who does not 'believe' in God, the supernatural or the religious. Kee argues that the biblical witness is that people experience transcendence *before*, and apart from, belief in God, and then 'God' is really just one way among many of speaking of the reality of the experience of transcendence—an experience which in our secular culture comes to us in varied aspects and experiences of our contemporary life.

In the Conference discussions, the question of God was felt by many to be a biographical matter. John Davies remarked that it was 'important to have somewhere in one's history that God is not what I had learned he was'. This could lead to atheism, or atheism for a time, or atheism as rejecting theism in order to get with what was meaningful to one as a stance of faith. The discovery and commitment of faith is a happening which makes a new story, which shows me who I am now. It is only by a piece of history in one's own existence that one can end in a statement about God: and that statement itself will make one say 'Where God is now'—and also *what* God there is. This certainly means that 'God' is a 'marker' which some will use and some will not, dependent upon their cultural situation and personal history. But the *experience* which some will label 'God' and others not, is the vital thing. And the experience is that of being exposed in certain gospel-filled situations, and entering into the new open door there before one. There has to be some experience in which the cross is met with, in which one faces the issue, '*That* is the Son of *God*: believe it if you dare', i.e. 'God is the Father of *that* man: now what do you think?'. Alistair Kee remarked that atonement is incompatible with Jesus' idea of God, and with Jesus' style of life: God *can* say 'you are forgiven' before the cross. The danger, again, is that a pre-Christian idea of a righteous God is imported into the Jesus story. We must begin to 're-create' God after the mind of Jesus —a task hardly yet begun.

At the end of the day, a new kind of 'Trinitarianism' must arise. The New Testament preached a radical theology only because it held to a radical Christology. 'No man has seen God at any time,' says John 1:18, 'the only begotten, in the Father's bosom, has made him known.' The Father, then, resides in the shadows, behind Jesus. We do not need to see him. Or, at any rate, we do not see him. All we see is Jesus. And all we need to see is Jesus. And all that the Holy Spirit needs to do is to 'take of the things of Jesus and show them to the disciples' (John 16:14). Our trinitarian formulae have confused us into thinking there were three Gods, or points of God, or three 'faces' (persons) of God. There are not. For Christians, there is only one: Jesus. Father and Spirit are merely there as hidden origin and operative principle to the central element: Jesus.

If this appears to state too little about the Holy Spirit in a time of growing Pentecostalism, ecumenical neo-Pentecostalism, and charismatic movements, then we must simply say that the *criteria* whereby 'the Spirit' is to be tested remain the same—that is, the criteria are *the marks of Jesus* and not primarily the interior witness of the Spirit or the external manifestations of Spirit-possession. Many in the charismatic movements would agree. But it is a matter of priorities which has not been heeded in all too many Spirit movements of the past. The Spirit takes the Jesus-things and extends their life. That is sufficient. It means we must ask, 'What are the Jesus things?' before we ask 'Where is the Spirit?'.

6. Politics as Gospel Action

'The *waste* of theological energy in Britain is just scandalous', John Davies told us at one of the Conferences. 'It is part of the conspiracy of evil to allow theology to trap itself in irrelevancy.' In Galatians, he said, Paul battles not with 'What is true?' but with 'What gets people moving?'—not doctrine is at issue, but with whom Christians can eat. It is religion of the heart plus political obedience, imagination plus commitment, situation plus action (see Davies's new Commentary).

It is no surprise that the majority of the groups we have referred to see their gospel-happenings as taking place within the area of secular action and activity. Some of the elements of contemporary 'strategy' referred to by Ed Kessler's paper are already manifesting themselves in a variety of political commitments and experiments. By 'political', we mean simply organized and sustained activity in public affairs: related to power blocks, classes, parties, races, community issues, social conscience, international issues or economics. Such actions must not be judged in terms of their assessable 'political results'—any more than the old devotional use of Jesus-stories could be judged by results. The story functions as a stimulus, a source of inspiration, or strategy, or technique in either the devotional or the political realm. It suggests lines of activity, methods of working. It offers built-in prejudices, biases, intuitions, perhaps methodologies. Sufficiently, it offers stories, themes and patterns that *people hear to be implying* specific commitments for them.

Roy Crowder's picture of modern young people's search for community indicates some of the basic preoccupations and assumptions of many contemporary Christians—internationalism, peace, permissiveness, participation, education, liberation. The list together describes some of the signs associated with the youth culture. All of them occur within all of the many and varied areas and cultures represented in our Conferences. What seemed to be now happening, however, went beyond this general mood. There is now a growing *specificity,* a persistence with small models, which takes one or two aspects alone (at least for a time) with complete commitment, at the same time as affirming in a general way people who shared the same 'spirit' but who are working at quite different aspects of the agenda.

To illustrate this would be to write a volume of contemporary Christian history. The evidence is only just beginning to appear, as people are only just getting their confidence back, to 'get into the Jesus story' through their political action. I confine myself here to a quotation from José Miguez-Bonino, which well illumines both the method of political-gospel-action, and also some of its problems.[13]

'Let me take an illustration from a very controversial person and situation in my continent: the Colombian priest Camilo Torres. He reads in the Gospel: "If you are offering your gift at the altar and then remember that your brother has something against you, leave your gift before the altar and go; first be reconciled to your brother, and then come and offer your gift" (Matthew 5: 23–4). He asks himself—using all the tools of knowledge available to him: who is my brother who has something against me? Not merely in an individual and subjective sense but as a priest who belongs to a particular historical structure of religious and political power, as an intellectual who belongs to a group who has played a role in history, as a member of a (economically powerful and dominating) class. The answer is clear: the poor, the worker, the peasant, he "has something against me". Furthermore, what he has against me is objectively real—my action in the solidarity of the institution, the group, the class to which I belong is an oppressive action. Therefore, if I interpret the text as merely affecting my subjective interpersonal relation to those whom I know personally (within the circle of my relations) I am rejecting and denying the real estrangement. My interpretation in such a case is an ideological occultation, bound to the interests of my class. I can only read the text authentically from within the recognition of the class conflict in which my relation to the largest number of my brothers places me. The command to "reconcile myself with my brother" can only be understood, therefore, as objectively demanding me to remove the objective alienation between my brother and myself.

117

We can perhaps question the course of action taken by Camilo Torres as he moves into political action and finally into the guerrilla. But this discussion misses (or eludes) the point: Camilo reads the text in and out of the explicit recognition of his total involvement as an historical man and re-acts his praxis (practice) out of the total impact of the text on his involvement. He refuses to take refuge in a "normative" course of behaviour which would be found in the text without exposing himself to it, without bringing to it his total present reality. Otherwise he might have been satisfied to fulfil the "normative requirement" within the self-understood limits of his un-exposed and therefore unchallenged sociological condition (i.e. resolve the personal quarrel he may have had with a fellow-priest or a colleague-professor). And he refuses to let the command hover over the concrete historical circumstances in which his actions take place. Otherwise he might have been satisfied with an action of charity—which leaves the objective conflict untouched. Only by incorporating his action within a total "praxis" in which the cause of "offence" might be objectively removed could the reading of Jesus' word be actually "heard". Naturally, the relation between interpretation and praxis understood in this way, requires the use of all the analytical tools at our disposal—both in the understanding of our present praxis, of the text, and of the conditions for a new praxis. This is precisely the "theoretical" work. And this is the only justification for doing theology when it fulfils its task!'

7. Liturgy as Gospel Rehearsal

The relevance of our view of Christianity to politics may appear more clear than its relevance to the interior life of Christian communities. But our Conferences did not ignore the question of liturgy: Catholics present ensured that.

Once Christian communities can be liberated from unreasonable and un-gospel-like expectations of themselves, the theology being urged is extremely instructive. The little self-conscious group of intentional Jesus-followers may not themselves often be the *locus*, much the less the cause, of the actions of faith. But it can be the place where those actions are expected, hailed, forwarded and seen for what they really are. Liturgy is *rehearsal* of the whole story of *Jesus'* ministry, passion, death, resurrection; Liturgy is 'doing something together' in the light of the gospel. The faith-life of Christians actually *proclaims* the gospel to the world. Christians need the liturgy to re-establish themselves as being what they are, the people named by and described in the story, and thus celebrate themselves as those who have a place in history, and who have a meaning beyond their own meaning. In Donald Tytler's words, they are 'free to celebrate'. Liturgy is a two-way process. *Worship* is from a low being to a high being; but a *liturgy* can be between equals—doing something together. It is a work of a group acting together, passing the story and its symbols from one member to another in word or music or action. Originally, Tytler added, the word *leitourgia* could mean the contribution made by citizens towards the maintenance of their city, especially in time of war—like our income-tax. It was an action intended to preserve the people's security, as the ancient rituals did. It was a secular community action which cemented belonging.

Given that the gospel story produces action, and people have lived their lives out of what was for them in the gospel, or what grabbed them from the gospel, then there will be *testimony* about their action. The way they see it afterwards will be different from the pure event; it will be recollection tinged with faith-interpretation; and that is testimony. The 'question' of liturgy is therefore a vital question. What could a group of Christians do, who wanted to (1) Thank God for *their gospel-type action*, about which they have testimony; (2) Thank God for *the gospel itself,* which is the myth informing their understanding; (3) Confirm each other in their 'mythical' gospel-understanding; and (4) Drive each other into conscious gospel-expectation and action? What would a group do that wished to push along this mythical self-understanding? What words or actions (even 'preaching' or 'sacraments') would they perform for each other? These are the questions to be asked about liturgy.

Such questions in our time are creating experimental eucharist groups. In many places, there are 'eucharistic groups' up and down Britain, of a non-church or para-church kind, which seek to 'gather strength and gain depth to our life together, through meeting, letting the Bible speak to us in our new situation, through celebrating this new life and through passing the bread and sharing the wine'.[14] I have elsewhere described the Sheffield Sunday Lunch Eucharist.[15] In each case, groups create their own liturgy, as they do within the Roman Catholic groups which are found in the para-church.[16]

All this hails a new development in the radical 'camp'—*the emergence of confidence.* Radical theology can disturb and challenge. But this is not its function for many people. For many, after ritualism, death of God, or death of old faith, radical theology is a form of *reassurance.* After doubt and despair, radical theology comes as a way of asserting the taking of the gospel out of the arena of dead questions (denominations, futures, hymns, disciplines, *bêtes noires*) into the arena of real gut issues—death, life, despair, hope, self-seeking, vocation, affluence, self-giving. And it is natural that those who find it so should now express themselves *liturgically*.

The group of the friends of Jesus when they come together thus both act and speak. The work of Jesus is the first *leitourgia*, and so itself the creation of the new, both in himself as New Adam, and in us as the firstborn of many brethren. Our *leitourgia* is our work in the light of the work of Jesus. So the eucharist in fact constitutes the alternative society—the eschatological community. Eucharist is an *ideal* (someone in one of the Conferences said), a *hope*, and a *voluntary subscription-list*. The Church is the *sign* of the kingdom, and sets up images of the universe full of justice and peace, which is being fully human. The institutional churches and denominations, of course, have the theology for and the expectation of all this. And, of course, it often happens there. But when it does not happen there, or happen often or significantly or relevantly *enough*, the institutional churches must learn to rejoice that it is also happening alongside them.

8. Making Disciples

Much theology in England has been concerned with providing rational justifications for Christianity; but it has made few converts. Converts have been made by charismatic figures—high church, pentecostalist, evangelical, Roman Catholic, or whatever. But the theology, pristine in clarity and impeccable in logic, has converted very few. Nor yet could one expect that such theology would or could ever be 'evangelistic'. Now, we have broadly defined theology as 'what Christians do when they work at the Gospel in their own context'. Theology is, obviously, a 'believer's' occupation. Nor yet do we think our book is essentially different. But it could open up one or two new possibilities for Christians.

First, it invites people to get with the gospel story and let it speak to them. It does not argue that the story is the most obvious or the most compelling account of the nature of things that could be imagined. It says, 'Get in on this story and try it on for size'. By this, it means also 'try out a few gospel-style actions and get into some gospel-style groups'. It invites readers to expose themselves to the Jesus phenomenon, in words, in deeds and in people.

Secondly, it invites people to come to Jesus without too many presuppositions. Of course, no one can do this completely. The sociology of knowledge, indeed, suggests that beliefs function in very predictable, culture-determined and culture-affirming ways. Whether or not one encounters belief in God as an option depends upon whether or not one comes into contact with a religious culture. Most people alive in the world today do not encounter belief in God. In Britain, more and more people every year grow up more or less completely out of touch with a religious culture. Our claim that the bits of religion surviving in that culture will not prepare them for Jesus-faith is a separate argument. In either case, there is an enormous problem of evangelism. Can we find new ways of raising the questions of meaning, ultimacy, value and significance in a post-religious culture? Can we find new ways of indicating Jesus in a world which does not believe in God, or whose God is incompatible with Jesus? Can we find ways whereby people can be discipled to Jesus without necessarily taking on the whole of first century theism, the whole variety of Christian traditional theisms, and the contemporary establishment 'God'?

Thirdly, it invites Christians and theologians to ask whether what they are 'on to' is really Christianity. We have set out lines for a few vocations for theologians and Christians. We are going to try to follow them ourselves. We think discipleship to the Jesus we see is something worthwhile, and comprehensible, and compelling. Things are stirring. The endeavour is making disciples. Even theologians can come. bringing their gifts. Even churchgoers, bringing theirs. Even unbelievers, bringing theirs.

Notes

1. See the account in *Search for Gospel, New City 6*, Spring 1974 (Sheffield: Urban Theology Unit).
2. Cf. *People's Church: Directory of Christian Alternatives* (Wick, Bristol: Student Christian Movement, 2nd ed. 1974).
3. Walter Hollenweger, 'Pentecostalism', a lecture delivered at the August 1973 meeting of the Oxford Institute of Methodist Theological Studies.
4. Cf. my chapter on 'Innovation in Great Britain: The Sheffield Urban Theology Unit', in *Learning in Context*, ed. Shoki Coe (Bromley, Kent: Theological Education Fund 1973), pp. 116–31.
5. *Theology in Action*, ed. Jae Shik Oh and John England (Tokyo and Perth: East Asian Christian Conference, 1972).
6. Cf. *Struggle to be Human*, ed. Bobbi Wells Hargleroad (Geneva: World Council of Churches 1974).
7. Ian M. Fraser, *The Fire Runs* (London: SCM Press 1975).

8. David Blatherwick, *Adventures in Unity* (London: British Council of Churches 1974).
9. John J. Vincent, 'The Sheffield Inner City Ecumenical Mission' (London: One for Christian Renewal, March 1975); Roy B. Crowder, ed., New Wine, New Wineskins; *New City 9*, October 1975 (Sheffield: Urban Theology Unit).
10. Edward S. Kessler, 'Planning: A View from Below' (see ch. 1, note 6).
11. We lack a study of the similarities in Gospel elements presently found in these two contemporary phenomena of the churches. Meantime, I agree with Walter Hollenweger that they, between them, constitute perhaps the most hopeful signs in the churches at present.
12. Cf. *Black Theology: the South African Voice*, ed. Basil Moore (London: C. Hurst & Co. 1974); *A Theology of Liberation*, Gustavo Gutierrez (London: SCM Press 1974); *A Reader in Political Theology*, ed. Alistair Kee (London: SCM Press 1974), and references there.
13. José Miguez-Bonino, 'Marxist Critical Tools: Are They Helpful?', *The Politics of Bible Study* (Wick, Bristol: Student Christian Movement 1974), pp. 9–12, p. 11.
14. Alistair Kee, in *Seeds of Liberation* (London: SCM Press 1973), p. 114.
15. John J. Vincent, 'How I See the Eucharist', *Worship and Preaching*, 6, 3, June 1976;
also 'Search for Church', *Act* (Ashram Community Trust), 8, September 1974, pp. 5–12.
16. Cf. my forthcoming *Alternative Church* (ch. 1, note 6, above).

NOTES ON AUTHORS

ROY B. CROWDER. Born in 1947. Lived most of his life in Methodist manses near the centre of northern industrial towns with the exception of Bilston, Staffordshire—a Midlands industrial town full of heavy steel works. Schooled first in Saltaire (first planned milltown in Yorkshire), then at Wolverhampton Grammar in leafy suburbs. Read English—intermittently—at St Peter's College, Oxford, where he almost gave his life to punting and conversation. While teaching in a Leicester grammar school lived among Asian immigrants in Highfields and began involvement in community action. Re-educated by dropping out of school and into Liverpool Petrus Community for homeless people. Living with dossers for a year challenged his Oxford English vocabulary and feeble politics and confirmed his move towards a radical understanding of Christian commitment. Moved back to Sheffield Ashram Community House in 1972 to continue work in community and try to think through what had happened by studying in UTU, where he now lectures.

JOHN D. DAVIES. Born in 1929. Left Britain in 1956 with his wife Shirley to work in South Africa, in the Transvaal and Zululand, 1956–62, then in Johannesburg as chaplain at the University of the Witwatersrand and the College of Education, 1962–70. Was a Founder-member of the Board of Management of the Christian Institute, was chairman of the University Christian Movement Formation group, and was involved in the 'Message to the People of South Africa' (1968). Visiting Britain in 1970 with his wife and three children, was prevented from returning by restrictions imposed by the South African authorities, and joined the staff of the Church of England Board of Education, with responsibility for higher education chaplaincies, where he served 1970–4. Is now a Chaplain at Keele University and Vicar of the Parish of Keele. He sees many symptoms of apartheid in Britain, developed from systems and attitudes which have been flourishing for centuries, and hopes the gospel can be a fundamental disturbance and give new hope to the oppressed. Publications include *Beginning Now* (Collins), and *Good News in Galatians* (Fontana).

123

EDWARD S. KESSLER. Born in 1926 in Newark, New Jersey. Trained in politics at Princeton University (B.A. 1947) and in planning at the University of Chicago (M.A. 1951), he followed a varied career in town planning from 1952 to 1964 when he came to St Chad's College, Durham, to train for the priesthood in the Church of England. Ordained Deacon in 1966 and Priest in 1967, after working as a curate in a number of parishes, he became Planning Officer of the Diocese of Durham in 1970. As Planning Officer he has taken stands with ordinary people in slum areas and small villages in the North-east against what he sees as the oppressive effects of much planning. He is also Priest-in-charge of Kimblesworth, a mining village in Durham Diocese. Joining Urban Theology Unit in 1973, he is now Associate Director, and commutes between Sheffield and Durham, dividing his time between teaching in UTU, training ministers, consulting in parishes, and running around his parish.

DONALD TYTLER. Born in 1925. A radical within the Establishment. With a down-to-earth approach that follows from twenty-five years work in Birmingham, he believes that honesty in religious belief is vital for the health of the Church. This conviction goes back to his time as Chaplain in Birmingham University, 1952–5, when he had to answer students' questions, reinforced by seven years as Director of Education for the Birmingham diocese, 1957–63. At this time he wrote a secondary school text-book, *Operation Think*, that broke new ground with an open questioning approach to religious education. Vicar of St Mark Londonderry and Rural Dean of Warley, 1963–72. Since 1972, a residentiary canon of Birmingham Cathedral, helping to find a contemporary role for a cathedral set in a great industrial conurbation. He recently completed two years as Secretary of a Commission studying Needs and Resources in the Birmingham diocese, published as *Structures for Mission*, which has made radical suggestions for new structures that will assist greater interdependence between local churches.

JOHN J. VINCENT. Born in 1929. After training for the Methodist Ministry at Richmond, London, studied New Testament at Drew and Basel. with doctorate under Cullmann, Reicke and Barth in 1960. Worked in city missions in Manchester (Wythenshawe), 1956–62, and Rochdale, 1962–9. Taught at Boston University and New York Theological Seminary, 1969–70. Went to Sheffield in 1970 and set up the Urban Theology Unit, now a part of the Sheffield Inner City Ecumenical Mission. His hobby is setting up organizations for freedom for prophetic concerns, from North-West Campaign for Nuclear

Disarmament in 1958 to the Renewal Group in 1961 to the Pitsmoor Action Group in 1970 and the Alliance of Radical Methodists in 1971. Has written on the gospels (*Secular Christ*), politics (*Christ in a Nuclear World, The Race Race*), and popular theology (*Christ and Methodism, Here I Stand* and *The Jesus Thing*). His much revised doctoral dissertation *Disciple and Lord*, is expected in a year or two. *Alternative Church* appears later this year (1976).

NOTE ON THE URBAN THEOLOGY UNIT

The Urban Theology Unit is an association of people committed to the problems of the city from a Christian point of view.

The Unit's main base is located in an area of change and diversity, in Pitsmoor, Sheffield's northern inner city. It is based on the Pitsmoor Study House, which was opened by the Unit as a community adult education facility. There is also a Library and Periodicals Room open to all.

The Urban Theology Unit functions in a number of related ways:

1) *Staff.* There is a small, but growing, part-time staff of people with a variety of skills and experience in theological study, practical church engagement, education, community work, community development, social problems, and 'alternatives'. The staff engage in teaching, research, consultancy and outside lecturing.

2) *Post Graduate Year.* There is a group of six to twelve students each year from October to June who form the Post Graduate Year. They come from many countries and have varied academic backgrounds and experience. They join in the ongoing work of the Unit, seek to help where they can in wider projects, and study urban issues, theology and vocational questions.

3) *Consultations.* Consultations are held each year, concentrating on special problems. During 1975–6, these were on 'Deployment for Mission', 'The South Yorkshire Structure Plan', 'Sociology of Theology', 'Urban Mission in Global Perspective', 'Urban Industrial Mission', 'Alternative Planning' and 'Urban Alternatives'. Study Weeks are also held on a variety of themes, and weekly evening classes are held, usually jointly with the LEA or WEA.

4) *Urban Ministry Courses.* In twelve cities, courses for ministers and others are held over 2-year periods of part-time work, mainly in the city concerned, plus a residential period in Sheffield. The courses mainly cover analysis of ministers' situations, plus theological reorientation and work at participants' programmes, with relevant special material as needed.

Membership. There is a Membership of several hundred ministers and lay people all over Britain who support the work of the Unit by subscribing at least £3 annually, or £5 for Friends, or £10 for Founding Members. Many of the Members covenant their giving. Members receive the two issues of *New City* published annually, together with other reports, Consultation details, and Study Project plans.

For full details, write: Rev. Malcolm Stringer, Registrar, Urban Theology Unit, 210 Abbeyfield Road, Sheffield, S4 7AZ. A 'sample bundle' of recent material will be sent for £1.